The Future of Navajo Education

Vol. 2

Published in the United States of America.

Fielding University Press is an imprint of Fielding Graduate University. Its objective is to advance the research and scholarship of Fielding faculty, students, alumni, and associated scholars around the world, using a variety of publishing platforms.
For more information, please contact Fielding University Press, attn. Jean-Pierre Isbouts, 2020 De la Vina Street, Santa Barbara, CA 93105. Email: fup@fielding.edu.
On the web: www.fielding.edu/universitypress.

Library of Congress Cataloging-in-Publication data
The Future of Navajo Education Vol. 2
1. Education – Higher Education – Navajo Education

The Future of Navajo Education

Vol. 2

Edited by

Barbara P. Mink and Miranda J. Haskie

Contributors

Albert L. Haskie
Miranda J. Haskie
Viola Hoskie
Perry R. James
Henry H. Fowler
Perphelia Fowler
Rose Graham
Pandora Mike
Buu Nygren
Telletha Valenski

Table of Contents

Fig. 1. Dr. Barbara Mink hosts the Fielding Graduate University booth during the National Indian Education Association Convention.

Preface

Rose Graham
Director of the Office of Navajo Nation Scholarship
and Financial Assistance

The future of Navajo education has significantly improved with the support of Fielding Graduate University for the Navajo Nation. This second volume of *The Future of Navajo Education* series covers stories of some of the most creative and innovative educators on the Navajo Nation.

The Future of Navajo Education is indicative of the new and transformative ways that Navajo educators explore the dynamic educational resources available in their communities and the world outside the Navajo Nation to propose organizational change in their areas of expertise. This book includes scholarly research that fosters social responsibility and community service in accordance with the educational philosophy of the Navajo people, Sa ‘ah Naaghai Bik’eh Hozhóón.

Fielding Graduate University offers a program to support Navajo educators to enhance their credentials by earning a Doctorate in Educational Leadership. The Navajo Nation’s partnership with Fielding Graduate University provides an opportunity for Navajo educators to earn an advanced degree without uprooting them from the communities where they are truly needed.

These Navajo doctoral students are able to study their own educational communities and also offer their research and findings at an annual research conference held in Window Rock. We are greatly appreciative of the invaluable support and guidance provided by Dr. Barbara Mink, Program Director, Education Doctoral Program. Through her efforts, former students and graduates are brought on as mentors and educators for students new to the doctoral program.

We appreciate her efforts to inspire conversations amongst students about how Navajo values could be merged with Western values. Also, Fielding's President Katrina Rogers met with Navajo Nation leadership and affirmed the University's support of providing a rigorous course of study to help Navajo educators make meaningful contributions to their schools, community, and in tum, the entire Navajo Nation.

The Navajo Nation, through the Office of Navajo Nation Scholarship and Financial Aid (ONNSFA), agreed to provide financial assistance to eligible students seeking a doctoral degree. Recipients of financial assistance commit to teaching or serving in leadership capacity within the Navajo Nation or at schools with a significant number of Navajo students for at least one year for every year they receive financial aid.

Graduates are already making significant contributions at their schools and within their communities. They were an integral part of ensuring that Navajo students continued their education through the pandemic. These educators recognize the vital role they have in promoting the principles embodied in Sa 'ah Naaghai Bik'eh Hozhóón.

We hope that this book will continue to inspire Navajo educators to seek innovative ways to instruct the Navajo Nation's greatest resource, our children.

About the Author

Rose Graham is the Director of the Office of Navajo Nation Scholarship and Financial Assistance and staff to the Navajo Nation Teacher Education Consortium in Window Rock, Arizona, which serves more than 10,000 Navajo students pursuing post-secondary education annually. Prior to this, Ms. Graham worked with the Navajo Nation Council for nine years as Legislative Services Director, Legislative Advisor and Navajo Language Interpreter. She also served on the American Indian Graduate Center's Board of Directors in various capacities as President, Vice President, and Secretary from 2010-2017. Rose holds a Bachelor of Arts in Humanities from Fort Lewis College. She is a member of and secretary of the Navajo Interpreter Association.

Fig. 2. Navajo doctoral graduates following the 2023 graduation ceremony.

Fig. 3. Navajo doctoral graduates following the 2024 graduation ceremony. At the far left are the co-editors of this book, Dr. Barbara Mink and Dr. Miranda Haskie.

Introduction

Miranda Jensen Haskie
2002 FGU Alumna, Diné College

In 2021, the first volume on the Future of Navajo Education authored by Diné doctoral graduates from Fielding was so successful that it resulted in this second volume. This book is again authored by Fielding alumni from the Navajo Nation with special chapters by Navajo Nation President Buu Nygren and Rose Graham, Director, the Office of Navajo Nation Scholarship and Financial Assistance. These Fielding Navajo graduates contribute their expertise in advancing Navajo education. Many of these graduates remain rooted in their home communities across the Navajo Nation. Still others educate Navajo students in border towns next to the Navajo Nation.

In each chapter, you will read about the continual application of time immemorial principles and practices of the Diné people relevant to Navajo education in the 21st century. These foundational principles continue to guide the Diné people. The authors in this second volume seek to apply these principles as educators and leaders of the Navajo Nation.

Chapter 2, "Personal Reflections on Prominent Navajo Traditional Leadership;" Chapter 4, "Navajo Numbers: *Nóomba 'Ákwíígíí*, Holy Air"; and Chapter 7, "Creating Positivity Using *Hózhó K'é*", reclaim traditional knowledge to inform their praxis. Authors remember the simple daily practices of our Diné ancestors that grounded them in *Hózhó* (balance, harmony, and peace). James recalls the sacred significance of place-based knowledge as he describes areas "...embedded with stories, songs, prayers and offerings...essential to the survival..." of the Navajo. He recollects how he could re-tell these stories he first learned from the stories his grandparents told him. He recognizes his responsibility to re-tell these oral stories to retain and pass on the traditional "...knowledge of history, preservation, survival, ceremonies and cultural stability." H. Fowler enumerates Navajo numbers and explains their cultural significance to the Diné people. In his discussion of Navajo numbers, he incorporates his application of Navajo cultural teachings associated with each. He reminds readers how mathematics is "embedded in every culture across the globe." P. Fowler continues her research focus on Navajo female leadership. She contemplates how applying *k'é* (clan relationships) in the workplace can achieve positive working relationships and even promote employee opportunities for growth.

I also appreciate the chapter about "Reflections on Efforts to Revitalize the Navajo language." Dance among students and teachers promote a fun learning environment reducing the inhibition among students as they learned the Navajo language. Teachers reflect upon how much freer they felt after dance and endeavored not to be held back "…from teaching my language, our language."

In Chapter 3, "Shattering the Glass Ceiling," Hoskie writes about the Diné teachings of *Sa'ąh Naagháí Bik'eh Hózhóón* that foster the attributes of grit, growth mindset and self-efficacy. She makes a profound statement that "the development of young brains should not be left up to chance." Parents, grandparents, teachers and mentors all help build up grit, growth mindset and self-efficacy in the youth. Navajo cultural practices like planting one's cornfield, prayer and storytelling are all ways to build up these attributes. In Chapter 5, "Navajo Teachers Weaving Navajo Culture into their Pedagogy," Mike presents the philosophy of her father, a Kindergarten teacher, about the three teachers in a child's life: 1) parents, 2) school teachers, and 3) environment. Her father firmly believed "children need to know who they are and where they come from to be successful in life." He inspired her to pursue teaching as a profession. She recommends a Navajo culturally relevant curriculum where Navajo students achieve academic success.

President Nygren affirms how Navajos have held onto our Navajo language and culture while embracing western education. He describes himself as a lifelong learner eager to meet the next challenge. He never wanted to be left behind and armed as a Modern-Day Education Warrior; he was determined to never quit and keep striving. Dr. Nygren looks forward to "what comes next" as Navajos "continue to hold onto our language and culture while integrating technology." A. Haskie and M. Haskie present the mobile app, *Adoone'e*, in their chapter. A. Haskie created the mobile app to help a younger generation of Diné learn Navajo clan relationship. M. Haskie reports data on Navajo use of digital technology as they access the mobile app, *Adoone'e*. These authors recognize the continual adaptation of the Diné people to not only survive but to achieve Navajo cultural resiliency in an ever-changing world. President Nygren adamantly states "to remain Navajo in a world of change and technology, we must invest in saving and promoting our language."

What I value about this book is how the authors' resume the vibrant Navajo oral tradition as they tell and re-tell the stories of their ancestors. James reminds us how the Diné story of the Hero Twin Warriors "...solidify one's leadership" and the teachings of *Táchééh* (Sweat House) convey traditional wisdom instrumental for Navajo leaders. President Nygren recounts the heroes in Navajo stories. The oral tradition of the Diné people continues. These oral stories retain the invaluable lessons of a people, the Diné people, whom stood steadfast grounded in the Navajo language, culture and traditions to rise above every challenge they encountered. These lessons remain as important today as they did for generations past.

There is a theme of storytelling in all chapters as the Navajo scholars reaffirm the importance of Navajo culture and language. These educators know Navajo identity through clanship, place-based knowledge and instruction support student success. President Nygren strongly encourages the pursuit of Navajo educational sovereignty. This compilation on Navajo scholarship to the literature is warranted.

Miranda J. Haskie is the co-editor of this book.

Chapter 1

Reflections on Efforts to Revitalize the Navajo Language

Dancing to Learn Navajo: Assessing Levels of Perceived Learning Enjoyment in Young Dual-Language Navajo Students Following a Short Session of Aerobic Dance

Telletha Valenski

Abstract

To improve both motivation and positive learning of the Navajo language for young Navajo children who are primarily English speaking, I introduced a dose of dancing before a typical Navajo language class for elementary students. The goal for the 15 minutes of dance was to create a sense of enjoyment that would carry over into the course, and the results were that students engaged. This study shows that traditional Navajo holistic education orientation that incorporates music; independent, free-flow dance; and exercise of the body prior to a language lesson can enhance learning outcomes. Although the experiment had a small number of participants, the positive results, coupled with my own experiences as revealed via autoethnographic interpretations, offer new directions for creative instruction on behalf of saving the Navajo language.

Postdoctoral Journey on Study

As I embark on my postdoctoral journey, I am captivated by the unique and transformative potential of the Diné-Centered Perceptive model. As illustrated in Figure 1, this model introduces a distinct clockwise approach to thinking. It challenges us to consider: What if a 10- to 15-minute session of aerobic dancing just before 3rd-5th grade Navajo language class could significantly enhance student enjoyment of the learning experience? Moreover, what insights can we glean from autoethnographic interpretations of the process and the outcomes? This innovative approach is impressive and holds great promise for language revitalization.

At the Math Circles camp at San Juan College, a fractal pattern seminar led to a profound realization. Fractal patterns, as elucidated by mathematician Maria Droujkova, can be a potent tool for analyzing and communicating complex ideas (Vedantu, 2023). This insight spurred me to consider how the practical application of the Diné-Centered Perspective could enhance the comprehension of the Navajo language for Students A, D, and E (subjects in research). This could potentially lead to moments of profound joy and satisfaction, as evidenced in my dissertation results. These moments, far from being fleeting, can be a consistent part of the learning process, instilling hope and optimism for the transformative potential of the Diné-Centered Perceptive model.

Similarly, the joyous moments the Creator has woven into complex ideas culminate in life, as it is the process of these moments. Over the years, numerous opportunities for enjoyment and satisfaction have been evident, as the Oxford Dictionary defines as a 'state of being happy,' with similar words including enjoyment, cheerfulness, and heaven (Merriam-Webster). These moments of pleasure, as experienced by Student D in the Intervention group of my dissertation, are pivotal in recognizing the occurrence of happiness. Student D attested, "The dance got my blood moving; it was fun." "Moving around and back and forth, fast, playing, and laughing." These joyful moments, like the emergence of a fractal pattern, illuminate some complex ideas I will delve into later in the paper, inspiring hope for the transformative potential of the Diné-Centered Perceptive model.

Similarly, Student A in the Nonintervention group responded, "It felt okay. I read the Dr. Seuss book." After the language instruction class, she was also the child who inquired, "Can I read a book out loud to you?"

She drew assumptive connections of when she had experienced similar enjoyable moments. How can teachers or scholars foster more opportunities for Indigenous students to experience "energizing" moments in learning other potential subject areas, "math, reading science, and even the Navajo language," as hinted by Student E in the Intervention group?

Changing the Environment

The excitement of the newfound joy in life questions started: Where does the enjoyability come from? What causes the link to experience moments of happiness? It was when I heard about fractals from Maria Droujkova that I made some associations based upon a tendency: "Languages are not merely a collection of words, but networks which can be displayed in n-dimensional spaces" (Ribeiro et al., 2023).

Similarly, the students in my research's intervention and nonintervention groups shared a familiar geometric concept: the Diné Centered Research process taught at Dream Diné Chart School (Werito & Belone, 2021) in Figure 1. Students were aware of "nitsáhákees" (thinking concept) as one of the first geometrical concepts by which research design was created to add a familiarity layer associated with root languages when the Navajo language was spoken. Also, students were able to engage with me on these questions that included:

1. How did you feel about your lesson today?
2. Did you enjoy the aerobic dancing today?
3. Did you enjoy learning more today than usual?
4. Was learning the Navajo language different from usual today?
5. Is learning how to speak Navajo vital to you?

Based upon the uniqueness of Dream Diné, I asked the above questions outside the classroom after the lesson on the Diné Language. The environment was enjoyable and culturally centered based on what *Nahatá* (planning and sharing concept) states. Students shared the "knowledge" they had gained in their language classes in a non-controlled environment. Student E went into planning mode, stating, "I want to see the teachers

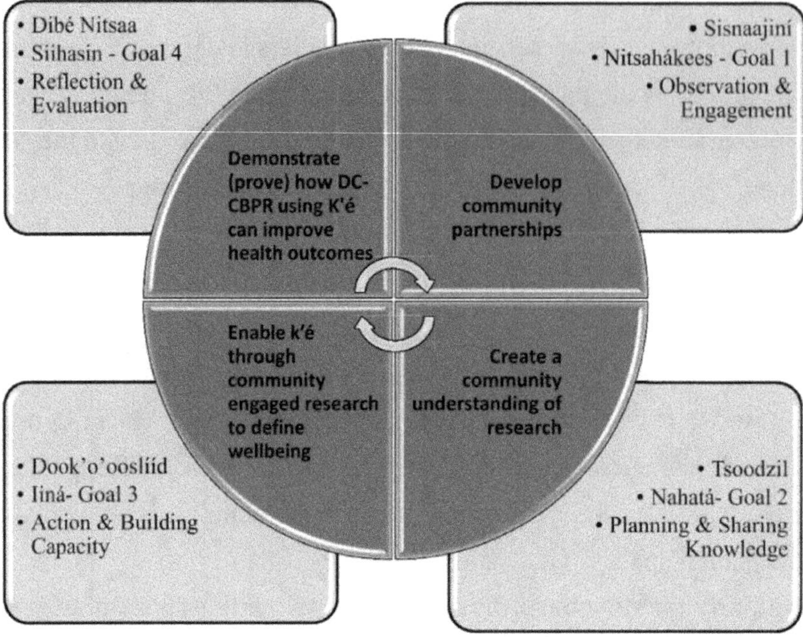

Figure 1. *Diné-centered research process using Diné educational philosophy.*

dancing and not just the students." The same Student E says to dance and exercise before each lesson to "energize" his brain to learn.

On the other hand, the teacher of the study states that she created a "happy environment," as found in the Diné-centered research process: Iiná. The teacher "built" a setting that allowed learning to be fun and happy, impacting student learning. She implied that students who engaged more in understanding the Navajo language said more of the Navajo words. She made her classroom a happy environment, like dancing the two steps. In building fluency in the Navajo language, students were encouraged to set their minds and goals to speak more Navajo according to the Diné-Centered perceptive process.

In the same way, using the Diné-Centered perceptive, the teacher naturally started making "observations and evaluations." She states, "I think, as an elder, we are not sharing with the next generation." She passionately said, "I do not want anything to hold me back from teaching my language, our language." She says, "I am glad I can speak, write, and read my Navajo language. I can understand the words, and it makes me so joyful. This joyfulness of teaching the language creates the enjoyment of learning the language. The knowledge comes from my grandparents and parents." Our elders create the circle to continue into the next generation.

Equally important, fractal properties of language reveal how living organisms interact with the classroom environment, just as Students A, D, and E, including the teacher, experienced (Ribeiro et al., 2023). There are hierarchical agreements that need to occur for that enjoyability to be transfused into their responses in learning the Navajo language. The link between each part in Figure 1 creates a "functional way " to achieve and complete excitation-inhibition processes systematically. (Ribeiro et al., 2023). Each segment contributes to a relationship between students and the teacher, allowing them to enjoy the process.

The fractal mathematical model helps explain the complex nature of the Navajo language. It provides a directional concept in the *Diné-Centered Perspective* that allows Students A, D, and E and the teacher to connect with each question to enjoy the process (Smith, 1984, p. 4). There is a formality that imposes importance in the formulation of the Navajo language to generate representation and interpretation of the words spoken. Smith states that "directionality is important" for most languages (Smith, 1984, p. 5). Therefore, I believe it impacted how the students and teachers related to the enjoyment of learning the language in the clockwise relationship.

Creativity

As Tustin (2018) states, "There is no reason you can't make it enjoyable" for students. Introducing a 10-15-minute dancing session can create a moment of enjoyment. The connection between the brain and muscles causes a form of engagement. Technology often consumes students' time, so dancing allows them to connect to the present state while learning the Navajo language.

In addition, Bucker (2013) discovered that the cerebrum and cerebellum play a direct role in motor function and cognition. The question I ask educators is, how does engagement play a role in learning? Learning involves the physical and mental faculties that engage in the learning process. While I taught physical education, I shared with my students that "learning begins in the muscles," whereas Barlie (2017) quotes Dr. John J. Ratey, "First it (exercise) optimizes your mind-set to improve alertness, attention, and motivation; second it prepares and encourages nerve cells to bind one another, which is the cellular basis for logging in new information." Motor function and cognition play a significant role in learning the Navajo language, such as dancing for 10-15 minutes before learning the Navajo language. This causes students to be motivated to learn in a learning environment like blended learning.

In addition, blended learning offers students different learning modes, including delivery, models, and styles (Kaur, 2013). The students in my study were offered 10-15 minutes of dancing before the Diné Language course while doing Zumba dancing. Students can do basic dancing moves by introducing "Just Dance" videos on YouTube. Also, the students had a Zumba instructor in their physical education course who helped with counting steps of four per dance move. Counting four steps coincides with the traditional way of Diné thinking to transition from dance to the Navajo language.

Conclusion

Classroom teacher and neurologist Judy Willis (2007) states, "When the fun stops, learning stops, too" (p.1). The keyword is enjoyability, which would create a continued sense of engagement. In early elementary, students often talk about what they learn and do in school. Still, the enjoyment of socializing, interacting in groups, or being creative in dance does not count as academics. This joy and ease creates an active learning environment. In the classroom, she has seen the benefits of pleasure in that studies have shown that neuroimaging and measurement of brain chemicals reveal comfort levels that could affect information conduction and storage in the brain (Willis, 2007). I want to support excellent teaching practice, like Willis's, by using the neuroscience of enjoyment to have the students engage and be motivated through the dance to allow information to flow into the learning of Navajo. Although Willis claims that when the fun stops, learning stops, my study shows this is not necessarily true because when the joy of dancing is over, the impact of the learning continues.

About the Author

Telletha Valenski is a graduate of the doctoral program at Fielding Graduate University. She is Diné from Whitehorse Lake, New Mexico. She is also one of many founders of Dream Diné Charter School. Telletha has been a school health education specialist for 18 years at Northern Navajo Medical Center in Shiprock, New Mexico and a governing council president for Dream Diné Charter School. Telletha has for many years worked as a trainer for the Sports, Play, Active, Recreation for Kids curriculum from San Diego, CA across the Navajo Nation. She has been engaged in advocating for language revitalization, public speaking at national, international, and local conferences, and as co-director of youth camps, organizer of school health conferences, while conducting training on financial literacy to community members and youth on Navajo Wellness Model, and children and youth advocate across the Navajo Nation, Argentina, Mexico, Northern Arizona University; Kilgoris, Africa, and Quetzaltenango, and Guatemala (Colegio Albert Einstein).

References

Barile, N. (2017). Exercise and the brain: How fitness impacts learning. *Western Governors University.*

Buckner, R. L. (2013). The cerebellum and cognitive function: 25 years of insight from anatomy and neuroimaging. *Neuron*, 80(3), 807-815.

Denetdale J. (2008). The long walk: The forced Navajo exile. *Chelsea House Publications.*

Kaur, M. (2013). Blended learning-its challenges and future. *Procedia-social and behavioral sciences, 93*, 612-617.

Morales, L. (2020). Navajo Nation loses elders and tradition to COVID-19. *National Public Radio.* https://www.npr.org/2020/05/30/865824083/navajo-nation-loses-elders-and-tradition-to-covid-19

Merriam-Webster. (n.d.). 174 synonyms & antonyms of happiness. In *Merriam-Webster.com thesaurus.* https://www.merriam-webster.com/thesaurus/happiness

Ribeiro, L. C., Bernardes, A. T., & Mello, H. (2023). On the fractal patterns of language structures. *Plos one,* 18(5), e0285630.

Smith, A. R. (1984). Plant, Fractals, and Formal Languages. *Computer Graphics, 18*(3), 1-10.

Vedantu. (2023, August 11). Fractal - types, structures, and examples. *VEDANTU.* https://www.vedantu.com/maths/fractal

Werito, V., & Belone, L. (2021). Research From a Diné-Centered Perspective and the Development of a Community-Based Participatory Research Partnership. *Health Education & Behavior.* https://doi.org/10.1177/10901981211011926

Willis, J. (2007). The neuroscience of joyful education. *Education Leadership,* 64(9). 1–5.

CHAPTER 2

PERSONAL REFLECTIONS ON PROMINENT NAVAJO TRADITIONAL LEADERSHIP THAT LED TO MY DISSERTATION

Perry R. James

My story in this monograph reflects a man's (my grandfather) desire to survive; live life to the fullest; have a healthy lifestyle; be self-driven; have confidence, courage, and strength; and continue the traditions instilled by his father. In the same way, I desire to survive; live life to the fullest; have a healthy lifestyle; be self-driven; have confidence, courage, and strength; and continue the traditions of my grandparents that led to the development of my dissertation.

Yikáiíhdą́ą́ (early dawn), my grandparents would start their daily routine. Their routine would almost always begin by constructing and igniting the fire in their home. *Kǫ'* (Fire) establishes the serenity of *Hózhó* (balance, harmony, and peace) in the mind, home, and the natural environment. In this early morning spiritual experience of *Hózhó, Shí Chei* (My grandfather J/W) would tell of sacred origin stories of the past and make connections to them about his upbringing. With a cup of hot coffee in his hand that he prepared by bringing water to a boil and adding ground coffee, he would begin to talk about open-ended topics. Today, I make my coffee the same way as he did to continue the traditions of how to make coffee, "The J/W Way!" Making coffee is one of many traditions I learned from him and continue to practice today in remembrance of him. During these early morning visits, I recall some open-ended topics about epic stories of the Hero Twin Warriors, Sweat House practice, the Fire, leadership, emanation stories, and self-identity revolving around the roles and responsibilities of men and women, and to self and others, to name but a few concepts. After my early morning trail runs, I would stop by my grandparent's house to visit and have some of my grandfather's coffee. He would first say, "Where did you run to, and how does the land look?" His question is what led to the nature of the problem, as I identified in my dissertation, and the specific outcomes that have engendered it.

With a cup of hot coffee in my hand prepared by him, I would tell him about the placed-based names of the areas where I did my morning trail runs. My familiarity with placed-based areas where I grew up as a child is places of sacred sites embedded with stories, songs, prayers, and offerings that relate to ceremonies, family history, ecological sustainability, and philosophy essential to the survival of the *Nihok'aa Diyin Dine'é* (Navajo). Placed-based areas are old remnants of hogans, sweat houses, corals, water sources, corn fields, offering sites, canyons, areas where medicinal plants grow, ridges, draws, archeological sites, boundaries of our homestead, and other places relevant to culture and respect. I learned of these placed-based areas from my grandparents while herding sheep, tending to cattle and horses, collecting medicinal traditional plants for ceremonies, hauling water from natural springs for drinking, and just out and about exploring and playing in the backcountry as a child. Ultimately, it was to understand our role and responsibility to the placed-based areas that instill knowledge of history, preservation, survival, ceremonies, and cultural stability.

Shí Chei placed great spiritual emphasis on the history of our homestead. He said that history tells us that the Holy People emanated all things and that the Holy Beings exist as inner beings in all things. Some examples of these Holy beings are as follows:

- *Diyin Dine'é Ndadildahgóó* – Traveling of Holy People
- *Nilch'i Diyin Dine'é Ndadildahgóó* – Air/Wind Travel through Space and Time
- *Ii'ni' Nahaz'ąągóó* – Places Where Lightening Has Struck Trees
- *Táchééh K'é* – Remnants of Old Sweat Houses

- *Hooghan K'é* – Remnants of Old House
- *Tsék'i nda'aashch'ąą'góó* – Petroglyphs/Pictographs
- *Anaasází K'é* – Ruins
- *Yeel ínídaal'įįgóó* – Offering Places
- *Kéyah Hane' Bidadiit'i'góó* – Oral History of the Land
- *Nahaghá K'ehgo Hane' Bidadiit'i'góó* – Stories Where Ceremonies Have Taken Place
- *Dził Naat'aah* – All Mountains are Considered Leaders
- *Tséyáłti' Daahólǫǫgoo* – Talking Canyons (Echo)
- *Ch'il azee'/Ch'il Ch'idao'ínígíí* – Medicinal Plants/Utilitarian Plants
- *Tó Dahnílínígóó* – Rivers and Washes

These examples are evident in the land I grew up on. *My Cheii* calls this having local knowledge infused and embedded with language, culture, place, ecology, making meaning, observation, sense of place, study, learning, knowing, application, spiritual dimensions, respect, responsibility, storytelling, traditions, and leadership. We (grandchildren) were taught to respect these placed-based areas of spiritual significance during these outings. As time passed, my grandparents advised me to teach my future children and grandchildren the same concepts and teachings of place-based knowledge. The teaching was to think in terms of the generations and what we are leaving behind for others as far as having a sense of place, a spiritual walk, planning, thinking, living life to the fullest, and reflecting, which leads to one's leadership and decision making in the well-being for all.

The generation I am referring to is a spiritual concept of *Táadi Są́ ná'oogáá* (three generations). Three generations exemplify our obligations to live life to the fullest, a healthy lifestyle, and longevity. These obligations are intended so that the current, especially the future generations, can thrive and benefit from all things created and established by past generations of the family. In essence, this is *Nihok'aa Diyin Dine'é* (Navajo) traditional leadership. In simple terms, three generations is a conventional leadership tool that guides one's thinking; planning; life; and reflection for oneself, one's children, grandchildren, and overall family. Three generations ask the individual, "What have you established that is prominent so that the current and future generations can benefit from your leadership?"

According to our family oral history, my great-grandfather is the first generation, *Shí Chei* (My Grandfather) is a second-generation prodigy, and my mother, aunts, and uncles comprise the third generation. My siblings and I begin the cycle of a new three generations, and we make up the first generation. With many blessings, our generations have lasted hundreds of years. The place I currently live, *'Ałch'í Hájisghai* (to converge together atop a divide in an open area), has been in our family for three generations and continues to be so to this day in 2023. As I run the trails and walk about in this place of stability today, I see the evidence of hard work, sweat, dedication, commitment, motivation, and courage of my grandfather's prominent leadership so that I could benefit from what he established.

One of the prominent pieces of evidence is the multiple green pastures secured by miles and miles of stretched fence lines for cattle range management. However, the evidence not seen by the average person is my grandfather's hard work; blistered hands; bruises; sweat; rising early every day; and commitment to digging, cutting, hammering, and tightening the fence. As a kid, I remember my grandfather always wearing a white t-shirt, brown felt hat, and boots while working and shaving cedar logs for the fence posts to be installed three feet into the ground. Shaving logs was one thing, but the hard work was digging three-foot holes for the posts. Most of the time, the land was so dry and demanding that he would dig about a foot depth and then add a bucket of water to the hole to loosen up the dirt to dig deeper and kept repeating this process until he reached a three-foot depth. To be sure, most of the posts have been in the ground for fifty-plus years. Today, as my uncles, nephew, brother, son, and I replaced the rotted wood posts, we talked about his hard work and the standard of installing posts three feet deep and we continued the same traditions. The evidence extends beyond the three-foot depth holes to the running of the barbed wire fence lines, which involved him and his carrying the 90lb roll of barbed wire to run the fence in the summer heat. My grandfather's hard work is a reminder and motivation factor for me, knowing that there is work to be done daily to continue the traditions of range management that come with the fundamentals of what fencing entails. Further, my grandfather's fundamentals of cattle range management are one example of his many prominent leadership activities still visible today on the homestead, which he established for me to benefit from in many ways.

Other examples of what he built that are prominent and still visible today are his traditional Hoogan, his Sweat House, his Corn Field, his home, his work areas, water wells, roads, and trails I see daily during my early morning trail runs; examples he built with his two hands. These prominent developments are how he defined traditional leadership. They are entities he used during his time, created for his children and us, the grandchildren. He left us important prominent landmark places like his Sweat House to conduct ceremonies for our well-being, a place to plant corn, a place to raise cattle, a place to sweat our bodies to cleanse our minds, body, and spirit, and a place to live with assurance and stability to continue to prosper and carry on the traditions he established. His vision for what he set was thought about, planned, and prayed into existence when he conducted a Sweat House ceremony embedded with many ancient teachings of our ancestors.

The Navajo cultural teachings that *Shi Chei* immersed himself in entail identity, language, family, cultural practices, ceremonies, spirituality, stories of heroes and heroines, songs, prayers, philosophy, responsibility to self and others, the role of men, having placed-based knowledge, and mental and physical fitness that defines traditional leadership. These are essential elements of self-actualization and traditional leadership in making effective decisions for the well-being of all. Mostly, my grandfather learned about these crucial elements in a spiritual environment, the traditional Navajo Sweat House.

In the spring of 2006, a year after my honorable discharge from the U.S. Army, a turning point in my life led to the construction of my Navajo Sweat House. It was a turning point that led me to believe in changing my way of thinking and self-actualization. The turning point was the birth of my son. I recall one morning visiting my grandfather after my daily trail run and told him that I wanted to construct my own Sweat House. After being still and quiet for a minute, he began to share stories about how he and his father would have Sweat House ceremonies. He talked about how his father would be away and that he would return in a few days and was instructed to have a Sweat House ceremony prepared upon his arrival. They would have the ceremony on the day of his father's return. Other men would accompany them who were invited. His preparations would entail gathering wood to heat the stones, gathering stones, medicinal herbs for emetic purposes, and water for drinking and bathing. He shared how he learned about these preparations through the epic oral storytelling of his father throughout their time together in the context of the *Naayéé' k'ehjí* (Protection Way).

According to my grandfather's traditional cultural knowledge, there are four distinct forms of spiritual wisdom: (1) *Hózhǫǫjí K'ehjí Hane'* – The Peace Way of Knowledge (2) *Diyin K'ehjí Hane'* – The Sacred Way of Knowledge (3) *Hatáál K'ehjí Hane'* – The Ceremony Way of Knowledge (4) *Naayéé' K'ehjí Hane'* – The Protection, Monster, and War Way of Knowledge. *Naayéé' k'ehjí'*, in theory, driven by genuine concerns and problems, portrays a series of events that are partly determined by the inner designs of the human heroic figures and divine characters involved and partly by the obstacles in the external worlds. Heroic figures like *Naayéé'neizghání* and *Tó bájíshchíní* (The Twin Warriors) are both noble and holy characters of prodigious strength who attempt feats that would be impossible for the average man, as narrated in the *Naayéé' k'ehjí'* way of knowledge. *Naayéé' k'ehjí'* foundation begins with the epic series of the Twin Warriors' events consisting of four major parts: divine birth, child rearing, journey to the Sun, and the killing of the monsters of the war way is a long epic oral narrative about the divine birth of two young boys' journey and the quest to save humanity. The divine solution was a war to end all wars, destined to decimate the vast numbers of Monster Beasts who were killing specifically young little children of the land. *Shi Chei* (My Grandfather) defines the two young boys as epic warrior heroes of prodigious martial strength and great courage infused with spiritual force. Their deeds to save humanity discover spiritual knowledge through their child-rearing, encounters with specific Spiritual Beings, the voyage to the Sun to acquire weapons from their father, the Sun himself, killing the monsters of the land, and sparing the lives of specific beasts. With assistance from supernatural forces, they venture into the unknown and eventually return home after a series of arduous trials. Overcoming the obstacles of the demanding trials came with endless preparations.

Before venturing into the unknown, *Naayéé'neizghání* and *Tó bájíshchíní* epic story, Part I, begins with their birth and child-rearing. This entailed two Spiritual guardians molding the young warrior boys mentally, physically, and spiritually to be solid and disciplined. In their childhood, the Twin Warriors' names at the time were *Łeeyánééyání* (Raised in the Underground). Running daily in the early mornings, providing for their mother was emphasized by their grandfather *Haashch'ééyáłtí'í* (Talking God). *Haashch'ééshzhini* (Dark Spirit God) made Bows and Arrows for them, taught them to hunt and be highly vigilant about their learning. These spiritual teachings are the early and beginning stages of the *Naayéé' K'ehjí Hane'* – The Protection Way Story. This teaching and molding are to identify males as young boys with mental strength outcomes that entail:

- *Azhdíltł'is* – Self-discipline/Prepared for Challenges
- *Na'ádizhnitaah* – Asserting Potential
- *Doo hoł hóyée'da* – Never be Lazy
- *Doo į'ni'jílįįda* – Do Not be Hesitant
- *Doo ni'na'azhdiilt'e'da* – Do Not be Unwilling, Resistant, Defiant
- *Doo ak'e jidlíida* – Do Not Feel Sorry for Yourself

With these immersed mental concepts, the young boys continued learning from other Spiritual guardians who knew what would entail their journey and empowered them to protect themselves from harm with specific instructions and spiritual fetishes in Part II.

Part II entails more instructions, learning, and earning and receiving spiritual fetishes required for their journey. Here, the epic story is famously known as *Hataa' Baazhni'ááz*: The Two Who Journeyed to the Sun their Father. Spider Woman knew the dangers of the trails and trials the young boys were about to ensue. After teaching the young boys about their journey, she gave them *Hinááh Bits'os* (Life Plume Eagle Feather). This Life Plummed Eagle Feather would protect and guide them to avoid and overcome deadly obstacles. *Nílch'í* (Light Breeze) enabled excellent communication skills by speaking into the inner ear of the young boys while instructing them on how to protect themselves and what to do to overcome deadly obstacles. When the young boys left the earth's surface using the Life Plume Eagle Feather to travel to the Sun, they traveled through the atmosphere. They encountered Thunder Storms, Dark Clouds, Dark Lightening, Dark Thunder, Dark Stars, Dark Hail, Dark Wind, and Dark Air on their way. As they journeyed, they spoke to and acknowledged the Deadly Thunder Storm and respected their Sacred names.

Before they left the earth's surface, *Wiishíyishii* (Caterpillar Elder Man) cautioned the young boys against the poisonous plants, tobacco, and the deadly sweat house ceremony they would be offered upon their arrival at the Sun's house. *Wiishíyishii* gave the young boys an antidote to protect and overcome by neutralizing the deadly tobacco. He also taught the young boys specific protection songs and sacred names of the fearsome creatures who protected the entrance of the Sun's house. By singing the protection songs and knowing the fearsome creature's sacred names, they overcame the obstacles without any form of fighting or resistance to entering the home of the Sun. The arduous journey to the Sun's house was merely about the young boys protecting themselves with spiritual fetishes and songs without harming or killing anyone. With the aid of the Spiritual guardians, songs, and fetishes, it is a spiritual concept referred to as *Bee Bits'á Honiyéé*. *Bee Bits'á Honiyéé*. The framework is for the young boys to rely on the child-rearing mental preparations they acquired, learning from the spiritual guardians who gave them fetishes and songs. *Naayéé Shísíih* is another terminology that means avoiding danger, destruction, and death. When used correctly and with respect, *Bee Bits'á Honiyéé* and *Naayéé Shísíih*, through songs and prayers, generate authority and power for protection through divination to combat anything that deals with opposing evil forces which the Two Who Journeyed to the Sun without ever having to fight or kill physically. The main objective for the journey was to acquire specific deadly weapons to kill the Monster Beasts on the earth's surface. Once they acquired the weapons, they returned home to the earth to commence the killing of the Monster beasts, which is Part III.

Part III is where the Twin Warriors physically kill the Monster Beasts using their spiritual body armor and weapons acquired from the Sun, their father, to achieve their objective. Part of the spiritual armor includes the mental concepts learned during their early child-rearing, the teachings and fetishes of the spiritual guardians, and the weapons they acquired from the Sun, their father. To have a better picture of this spiritual armor, they are as follows:

Child-Rearing Armor for Protection:

- *Azhdíltł'is* – Self-disciplined/Prepared for Challenges
- *Na'ádizhnitaah* – Asserting Potential
- *Doo hoł hóyée'da* – Do Not be Lazy
- *Doo į'ni'jilįįda* – Do Not be Hesitant
- *Doo ni'na''azhdiilt'e'da* – Do not be Unwilling, Resistant, and Defiant
- *Doo ak'e jidlíida* – Do Not Feel Sorry for Yourself and Pout

Spiritual Guardians Fetishes Armor for Protection:

- *Hinááh bits'os* – Life Plumed Eagle Feather
- *Naayéé' ach'aa sodizin doo sin* – Protection Prayers and Songs
- *Niłch'í* – Light Breeze Wind
- Sacred Names to Subdue the Fearsome Creatures

Body Armor and Weapons to Kill the Monster Beasts:

- *Atsiniłtł'ish K'aa* – Lightening Arrows that Strike in a Swerving Motion
- *Atsool'aghał K'aa* – Lightening Arrows that Strike in a Straight Motion

- *Shábitł'ool K'aa* – Sin Beam Arrows
- *N'aats'íílid K'aa* – Rainbow Arrows
- *Beesh Ch'a* – Kevlar Hat
- *Beesh Éí* – Kevlar Clothing
- *Beesh Doolghasii K'aa* – Dark Flint Knife and Arrowhead
- *Hatsolhał* – Stone Axe

Having spiritual armor played a significant role in the Twin Warrior's objective, mission, and success for the well-being of the people during a time of war. *Naayéé' K'ehjí Hane'* involves the Divine Birth, Child-rearing, Protection, Journey, and War that goes with killing the Monster Beasts. My grandfather learned that all young boys and girls, men, and women are leaders and that they should understand the epic story of the Twin Warriors. Knowing the story will solidify one's leadership in leading people to the well-being of all with effective decision-making. Of course, there is more to the epic story, a lifetime of learning the stories that any man will never achieve. Ultimately, part of constructing my own Sweat House was first to understand the stories, songs, prayers, and preparations to understand the purpose of the Sweat House truly. I thank my grandfather for sharing and showing me the *Naayéé' K'ehjí Hane'* path. Despite my little knowledge of the *Naayéé' K'ehjí,* I understand my role as a Man with many responsibilities to others, animals, the land, the natural environment, and myself.

My grandfather, uncle, and I had our first Sweat House Ceremony in the summer of 2007 in my newly constructed Sweat House. Learning about the essential Sweat House and the stories and songs accompanying the teachings took one year before my grandfather allowed me to construct my own. Today, my grandfather is no longer here to Sweat with me, and for the most part, I conduct the Sweat House ceremony alone with my son. However, I still reach out to my grandfather during my Sweats, where I can hear his voice and tell me how to prepare and remember all the stories he shared about how he and his father would Sweat together. Today, just as my grandfather did, part of my preparations for a Sweat House ceremony is waking early and gathering medicinal plants, which entailed identifying and locating specific herbs that pertained to the *Naayéé' k'ehjí*. The herbs' features consist of thorny sharp edges with a rough texture containing potent natural compounds to cleanse the inner organs and establish immunity to harmful diseases and sickness—gathering wood to heat the stones. Emphasis on proper stacking of the wood was a significant factor in ensuring the stones got extremely hot and would glow in the complete darkness of the Sweat House and getting water for drinking and bathing.

I am, moreover, spending the rest of the day remembering my time spent with my grandparents and teaching my son the traditions of the Sweat House ceremony, assuring his role as a young male with roles and responsibilities.

My Sweat House is a prominent reminder of my grandfather's leadership to continue the Sweat House ceremony practice traditions. If I had not pursued learning about the Sweat House practice, the tradition would have ended after my grandfather's passing. As I continue to learn traditional cultural practices, although my grandparents have passed on, their presence is still felt in many ways now and forever. My time spent with my grandparents has influenced my life and shaped my character. I know it has made me the person I am today. Through my grandfather's prominent leadership and teachings of the *Táchééh*, which entail learning about self, identity, discipline, preparation, manhood, warrior ethos, leadership, and spirituality, I have better understood how to live a good life. It has taught me how to respect ecological systems and know my authentic self, and according to my *Chei's* upbringing, such knowing comes from the heart and mind. Such knowing also helps me understand multi-faceted truths, reject falsities, accept the mysterious, and always do my best to walk with Hózhó, the concept of balance, which is the *Nihook'áá Diyin Dine'é* (Navajo) way of life. Considering the out-of-balance lives of so many people in the Navajo Nation and throughout the world, I wanted to share this knowledge to help make the world a better place.

The Nature of the Problem, as Identified in my Dissertation

My grandfather's prominent leadership is very noticeable and stands out to me. As I work around the J/W Ranch and make my daily morning trail runs, I see the fenced grazing pastures, his traditional Hoogan, Sweat House, Corn Field, home, work areas, water wells, roads, and paths that all exemplify what he built with his two hands. He made living on the Ranch easy for me in many ways, and the structures remind me of my role and responsibility as a grandson. My part is to continue learning from my uncles and about my grandfather through their stories about how they grew up. This learning will further solidify my responsibilities in continuing the traditions of the three generations and continue to build on our J/W Ranch for future generations of family.

Through sharing my stories of my grandfather, I have transmitted his Navajo cultural way of thinking in the first half of my monograph on how my dissertation evolved. Making my daily morning trail runs, visiting my grandfather after my run, and being asked, "Where did you run, and what does the land look like?" His question was a critical thinking question, and it shaped my dissertation in many ways. Despite my grandparents passing on before I started my doctorate studies in the fall of 2018, my grandfather's question, "Where did you run, and what does the land look like?" is always in my thoughts as I run the trails today. On one morning run, his question led to my dissertation research problem topic. The problem I identified in my dissertation addressed, in essence, relates to my belief that many Navajo leaders have lost their traditional teachings in ways that are stifling efforts for optimal well-being for all. I posited this mainly because our leaders have forsaken the Sweat House teachings, which entail learning about self, identity, discipline, preparation, manhood, warrior ethos, leadership, spirituality, and living a good life. The Sweat House is a conventional leadership tool used in the home, family, school, workforce, political arena, society, and life. I wrote my dissertation with the hopes that our Navajo leaders return to the traditional Sweat House teachings about leadership so they might be more effective in helping bring balance back to our people and prevent the loss of language, identity, culture, and traditional ways.

The problem I identified relates to conforming to mainstream culture and is one of many reasons our Navajo Nation leaders abandoned their cultural teachings. The mainstream culture of the existing leadership approach currently guiding the Navajo Nation reflects European hierarchy conceptions. Other examples of Navajo traditional leadership principles that are being lost today due to ideals of Western culture include social media, technology, food, drugs, alcohol, health issues, education, philosophy, and fundamental divergence in worldviews, to name a few of many reproachful problems. Therefore, such ideals make Navajo Ways of Life seem arcane, outdated, and impractical in modern times. Further, I believe most contemporary leaders have lost their Navajo identity by losing the traditional teachings due to divergence in worldviews. From a Navajo cultural perspective, being Navajo means language fluency, understanding one's clans, knowing the sacred songs/prayers, participating in ceremonies, and staying mentally and physically fit. Most importantly, language loss indicates that most Navajo have gone astray from the original sacred path created and intended for us since immemorial to continue the growth process for our future generations.

These reproachful problems have further led to a loss of *Nihookáá Diyin Dine'é* (Navajo) identity, and many seem to no longer see our worldview as sacred and ourselves as holy human beings. Our identity and leadership roles as *Nihokáá Diyin Dine'é*, men and women, are clearly defined at *Táchééh* (Sweat House) and play an influential role in life that can prevent such harmful acts. Further guiding our people toward a more sacred view of self, others, life, ecological sustainability, and the *Nihookáá Diyin Dine'é* way of living it; with this guidance, when learned and internalized, such harmful acts could then be eliminated. In my dissertation, I analyzed traditional stories and songs to explain how our current leaders can use them to combat alcoholism, obesity, sickness, poverty, leadership deceit, and domestic violence. In one example, through storytelling, I explained how the six sacred mountains still serve as our leaders today as protectors, are stable, give us a sense of guidance and direction with purpose, and can bless us when we sing and tell stories of their purpose. Sadly, today, our Navajo Nation leaders no longer, as a whole, protect us, bless us, guide us, give us direction with purpose, give stability, give life and well-being, serve us, and plan for our future. Because of this, they cannot spearhead resolving the problems of the Navajo Nation, much less overcome the problem's obstacles.

I submit that this is why some current Navajo leaders have not achieved sufficient goals for the Nation. Ultimately, if our current leaders want to solve issues plaguing our people, they will remember that within *Táchééh* (Sweat House), the solutions to our problems and answers are there waiting. I also explained how current and past administrations of the Navajo Nation have stressed the importance of restoring and revitalizing the Navajo language and culture. I contend that our government's actions too often contradict this goal. For example, the Navajo Nation owns and operates a coal mine and extracts natural resources from *Nihoosdzáán Nihimá* (Our Mother Earth), desecrating our fundamental four sacred elements (Earth, Fire, Water, & Air) in Her.

Another example is how Navajo leadership has lost its connection to traditional Navajo ways and how Western influence guides more than Navajo ceremonies. This lost connection relates to two former Navajo Nation presidents who went to Israel to learn what would better have been learned already from traditional Navajo Medicine Men and Women's wisdom. Instead of consulting with them to build a more culturally reliable and healthy Nation, they went to Israel to learn about developing economic infrastructure and to learn about agricultural practices. In any case, I believe both Navajo presidents compromised the Navajo traditional place-based teachings by not seeking the counsel of Navajo Elders, Medicine Men, and Women as an alternate option to the Israeli government. To disregard such counsel and travel thousands of miles to a foreign land to seek strategies and teachings for building a stronger Navajo Nation is testimony to how fully the loss of Sweat House leadership wisdom exists in the Navajo Nation. This compromise is especially tragic regarding the goal of learning about agriculture! Navajo traditional Elders know the cultural aspects of agriculture in ways that no one else could offer. The cultural aspects of agriculture have continued to revolve around the hundreds of years of local observation and experience with the land and water's physical and spiritual aspects.

Agriculture is an understanding of how plants grow, that plants have to have sod to sow, water to nurture growth, air to breathe, and light for photosynthesis processes respective of the Four Sacred Elements of life in Mother Earth, Water, Air, and Fire. These sacred elements are why *Nihook'áá Diyin Dine'é* has a spiritual understanding and appreciation for corn, human life, and leadership in the same analogy in its fruition in growth and development. So, this is one-way that Navajo traditional Elders, Medicine Men and Women, who know the cultural aspects of agriculture, can offer what no other can offer. The Sweat House Ceremony is context, a place-based knowledge infused with spirituality, teachings, growth, and development for the well-being of all in the Navajo Nation. For the Navajo Nation, place-based knowledge should be the vision and efforts toward economics, infrastructure, and agricultural development efforts to help build a balanced, more reliable, and healthy Navajo Nation

Further, in my dissertation, I included how Navajo traditional place-based wisdom could have helped combat the COVID-19 crisis on the Navajo reservation. However, I contend that Navajo leadership failed the Navajo people in handling the Pandemic. I wrote how, in a writing piece in 2020, Clahchischiligi points out how the leadership early on was inadequate in ways that reflect the dismissal of traditional ways and understandings about the living situation of many at-risk Elders:

> The coronavirus, as of August 4, 2020, has infected 9,139 people in the Navajo Nation and killed 462, many of them elderly. Some elders weren't even aware of the free food deliveries were happening. They had no phone, television, or computer. Their contact with the outside world came from Navajo radio stations like KTNN. Some had no contact at all . . . The boxes were supposed to feed people for a week, but some only held enough for two days. Others included outdated toiletries that had expired in 2010. One source

> told me that she was so worried about the elders in her community that she often bought food for them from her own pocket. Attempts to reach Navajo Nation President Jonathan Nez failed. As a Navajo journalist, I have heard many stories of Navajo officials who stonewalled reporters or intimidated people who spoke out. Navajo Nation leaders often refused to answer questions from Navajo reporters and local media (although they showed little reluctance when it came to giving quotes to national media like CNN and the New York Times). (Clahchischiligi, 2020, pp. 8-10)

Such treatment of Elders by Navajo Nation leaders during a pandemic is one sign of why my dissertation calls for a return to our traditional values. For Jonathan Nez, only this time, reaching out to Elders was only a driving distance within the reservation than traveling to Jerusalem, Israel. This treatment of Elders is another example of how far Navajo leadership is from traditional *Nihook'áá Diyin Dine'é*. Not only are they neglected, but tribal employees are also in the fray when they speak out against such treatment and were expected to remain silent while our Elders were dying during the Pandemic. Meanwhile, our Medicine Men and Women were forgotten and left out despite hundreds of years of evidence that our traditional ceremonial healing practices work.

Disregarding our traditional medicine was even being rationalized by Navajo leadership. In a piece written in the *Navajo-Hopi Observer,* it stated, "A $1 million set-aside for the Diné Hataałi Association was removed because it does not comply with the federal guidelines for using CARES Act Funds" (Locke, 2020, p. A1). "President Nez argued that Navajo medicine men and traditional practitioners were not explicitly allowed in law passed by Congress nor guidelines from the U.S. Treasury" (Locke, 2020, p. A2). In not being allowed to receive funding, the *Diné Hataałii* Association released a statement in response to the Navajo Nation president's line-item veto as follows:

> The *Diné Hataałii* Association is, in reality, the first responders and essential front-line public health workers who have always

> assisted the Navajo Nation, as expressed in the statement. Further, the association shared, "Unfortunately, those who are not in tune with Diné cultural and traditional ways do not understand the role of the DHA and its members in maintaining the overall wellness of our people and the Nation". . . Nez and Lizer authorized legislation 0116-20 with a line-item veto of an amendment justified by some Council members that would have provided $1 million in CARES Act funding to the DHA. The funding would have allowed the DHA to educate, share, and promote the teachings of *Diné* cultural wisdom and ceremonial healing practices . . . *Diné Hataałii* Association is the leaders and caretakers of *Diné* traditional cultural wisdom, ceremony, and herbal healing knowledge. We represent the original healthcare system of the *Diné* . . . "it is our sovereign authority for the *Diné* people to institute our own health solutions that meet their unique needs and to use federal funding to support culturally appropriate methods and tools for healing and restoration toward *Hózhó*," stated the DHA leadership. In addition to funding a broad, culturally appropriate public education campaign during the Pandemic, the DHA would have established funding for each region it serves with structured guidelines on providing financial relief and support certified *Diné Hataałii.* Our *Diné* people have experienced forced colonization for centuries with a resultant loss of knowledge of the language, culture, and traditional practices among our younger generations. *Diné* youth should be informed that they have cultural resources and traditions as a source of strength. The *Diné Hataałii* Association's statement closes with the following: "We did not think that we should need to explain or justify ourselves; instead, we expected Navajo leaders to possess and respect the intrinsic beliefs and knowledge of the essential and front-line work we do for and on behalf of the Navajo Nation." (Locke, 2020, p. A2)

The statements made by the *Diné Hataałii* Association in the last sentence of the above passage, "We expected Navajo leaders to possess and respect the intrinsic beliefs and knowledge," has been my argument for my dissertation. Sadly, most leaders then and currently do not possess and respect the intrinsic belief and knowledge of Elders, Medicine Men, and Women in instituting culturally appropriate methods for leading, healing, and restoring *Hózhó* (Balance) for our Navajo. Through the many years of survival, some individuals have continued to stay in tune with *Nihook'áá Diyin Dine'é's* cultural and traditional ways to lead the people thus far in utilizing the *Táchééh* to lead, heal, and restore *Hózhó*. However, the times have changed the early forms of leading, healing, teaching, learning, restoration, and disciplinary process of *Nihook'áá Diyin Dine'é*, as many have adapted to Western living. The conveniences of a simplified way of life, where people changed through attitude and behavior employing forced acceptance of a foreign culture's assimilation, are why most Navajo leaders do not possess beliefs and knowledge of the old ways. Having first-hand knowledge in *Táchééh* infused in leading, healing, teaching, learning, and restoration has led me not fully to assimilate. Therefore, I offered to current Navajo leaders and the world that the *Táchééh* is an excellent teaching tool to lead by all means, for the fact it bears fruition that produces humility, discipline, and determination in *Nihook'áá Diyin Dine'é* of contemporary times during the pandemic and other dilemmas we face together as a Nation.

In spearheading the many reproachful problems on the Navajo Reservation from a traditional perspective, with much hope, I believe my study's conclusions will help bring about the transformation that will help our leaders prevent such contradictions more soon in *Nihokáá Diyin Dine'é* society.

How I Investigated the Problem

My doctoral studies emphasized Education Leadership for Change with an elective choice in Dual Language. I was required to complete a theoretical dissertation, contributing new knowledge to various research areas. I wanted to use the Sweat House that I had constructed with the instructions of my grandfather's teaching and understanding of the Sweat House ceremony for my research. Moreover, I wanted to add new knowledge to the study of the Sweat House, which is still being widely studied in academia today.

My dissertation was entitled "An Autoethnography About Navajo Sweat House Leadership Teachings: Acquiring Traditional Identity for Restoring Traditional Leadership Perspectives." According to my literature review, the idea of using the Sweat House for leadership theory has never been approached or done. The purpose of my literature review chapter was to situate my analytic autoethnography in the related literature on Navajo identity, language, culture, traditions, ceremonies, and leadership. My goal was to make known common factors that establish support for my project and, more importantly, show how my research question addresses a gap in the literature from researchers who have studied the Sweat Lodge practices and the development of appropriate leadership skills attitudes. My literature review on the studies done regarding the Sweat Lodge had many positive intentions in an attempt for scholars to define and interpret its meaning and practice. However, I found no autoethnographic self-narrative had previously been done on leadership from this sacred context to this day. I demonstrated how my literature review about the Navajo Sweat House differs from most research scholars' studies on the Sweat Lodge. Through my findings, my research problem and question offer an authentic original contribution to the literature on the Navajo Sweat House and leadership. This validation led to my research methodology of orchestrating an autoethnography self-narrative to investigate my research question: "What learning and learning processes relating to the traditional Sweat House are relevant to Navajo leaders?"

My goal in this self-narrative was to show how the Navajo Sweat House serves as a source for learning how leadership is a daily Navajo Way of Life: It is a teaching/learning concept that develops authentically. It is about how leaders (all of us) can use each traditional teaching for optimal well-being for all; traditional teaching relates to the Sweat House Ceremony in terms of language, identity, our roles as males/men and females/women, meaning, spirituality, and the learning and learning processes of Sweat House leadership. As a self-narrative, I placed myself within a social context that aims more at prevention than postvention uses, for which I have found little research relating to leadership lessons and offers a unique contribution to Navajo and American Indian literature about this sacred ceremony.

Using my grandfather's knowledge and expertise about the Navajo Sweat House, I created a contextualized sense of sacred place, imagery, history, and philosophy throughout the research for readers by using an image in my dissertation of an ancient remnant of a Sweat House that is on the current property I live on. To help illustrate this sacred context and how it relates to the Navajo people, I shared many traditional stories shared by my grandfather, Elders, and Medicine Men/Women with me over many years using an autoethnographic self-narrative methodology. I did this with honest reflection and courageous words that describe real-life abstractions such as language, oral storytelling traditions, family history, teachings, stories of heroes and heroines, songs, and prayers, to name a few of the many important concepts required for optimal and effective leadership. I chose this methodology because what I share about traditional Navajo leadership is not found or rarely found in textbooks, articles, or websites.

I shared many experiences that influenced my life and shaped my character. The most important, however, were the encounters and spiritual awakenings from ceremonies. These awakenings were about one of the most important ceremonies, *Nihook'áá Diyin Dine'é bi Táchééhji* (The Navajo Sweat House Way Ceremony). Learning *Táchééh* practice serves a purpose for my life in many positive ways. Through the voyages of *Táchééh* learning, discipline, preparation, manhood, leadership, songs, prayers, and spiritual experiences, I have better understood how to live a good life, respect ecological systems, and know my authentic self. These experiences are the *Nihook'áá Diyin Dine'é* Way of living life. *Shi Cheii* (my grandfather), a man who spoke no English but only his Navajo language, is responsible for formulating my Navajo worldview. He had a vast knowledge of *Táchééh* and lived according to it. Learning about *Shi*

Cheii in different times and places has blessed me, and I am grateful for introducing me to his *Nihook'áá Diyin Dine'é* philosophy. His philosophy, built from his life's traditional elements (language, spirituality, songs, prayers, and ceremonies), embodies how to make sense of and understand life, oneself, leadership, land, and the world.

Ultimately, *Shi Cheii* fostered living in a world guided by spiritualism where the sacred can never separate from all else. He expressed this worldview to me at *Táchééh*. Although *Shi Cheii* has passed, I practice the *Táchééh* regularly, which has become an integral part of my life as a leader in progress. Considering the out-of-balance lives of so many people, it was vital for me to share his knowledge and way of life significantly to help Navajo leaders lead more authentically and effectively. In my doctoral dissertation, I attempted to transmit the practice of *Táchééh* leadership through interpretive autoethnography self-narrative experiences.

In chapter six of my dissertation, I narrated that in order for me to seriously undertake the Sweat House ceremony and practice knowledge, wisdom, and understanding of many other cultural aspects, I had a "responsibility" to construct my own *Táchééh* (Sweat House) in order to earn such knowledge. This undertaking of the Sweat House was also the birth of my son. Part of my entitlement was that I had to understand the meaning of *bá' atésht'į* (sacrifice). In this case, what was I willing to sacrifice to gain more knowledge? For one, I had to spend more time with my grandparents than ever before instead of hanging out with people and doing and learning nothing! *Ázhdíltł'is* (discipline) was another concept I had to grasp. *Ázhdíltł'is* entailed sitting for long hours in my grandparents' presence while they taught me the Navajo ways according to the Creation Story's oral traditions. *Ázhdíltł'is*, came with *t'áá biniik'eh* (willingness). *T'áá biniik'eh* tested my willingness to learn almost every day about the Sweat House. In learning about sacrifice, discipline, and willingness, the concept of *bíní'nlį* (determination) enabled me to construct my own Sweat House. Learning these four concepts enabled me *t'áá 'íít dįį* (readiness); I was now ready to build my own Sweat House. It took me over a year to learn just the general knowledge of the Sweat House before I was allowed to construct my own.

Following this milestone, *Shí Cheii* perceived me as worthy of learning more about the Sweat House practice and its intentions for almost everything. Worthy of in-depth knowledge included survival skills, ceremonies, stories, songs, prayers, medicinal plants, manhood, warriorhood, identity, hunting, leadership, husbandry, "kincentricity," Traditional Ecological Knowledge, duty, honor, respect, and integrity to honor our original Navajo culture for survival. Traditionally, in my dissertation, I explained how these survival skills can be emphasized in each of the four rounds intentions of the Sweat House teaching as follows:

I explained how the first round intends to emphasize respect for nature and its inhabitants—the songs and stories relate to how the Holy People assembled to construct the Sweat House and establish themselves. Here, teaching through songs and stories of Mother Earth and Father Sky introduces the concept of the four sacred elements (air, water, light, and pollen) that exist in all things and should be respected. The Elder, Medicine Man or Woman, then relates Mother Earth to one's biological mother, grandmother, aunts, sisters, nieces, and all women. It is the same for Father Sky. This way, women are respected, valued, and honored as leaders. Today, most Navajo men do not respect women; they are neglected, abused, and even murdered. Further, taking care of and respecting one's body, no tattooing/piercing of the body, acknowledging self as a male or female, daily hygiene is emphasized, and running early in the morning, being active, and attending to chores at home. This emphasis will enable a sound body, mind, soul, and spiritual thinking.

Intentions of the second round I emphasized nature's awareness, which takes a lifespan to learn. Men's and women's physical needs are dependent on medicinal plants, wild game food, and corn, which should be in one's daily consumption for survival. Sadly, this is not adhered to today in Navajo life; therefore, people have diabetes, cancer, obesity, consumption of alcohol, psychological problems, depression, and loss of joy. Songs about medicinal plants and rocks used for the sweat are acquired in the second round.

For the third round, I explained how it involves learning the Protection Way that centers around the Twin Warriors and entails living the warrior ethos to protect everyone. Songs that pertain to the eagle, horned toad, lightning, dark clouds, dark wind, mountains, and rock minerals, which are leaders, are instilled for guidance and protection to avoid chaos, danger, and destruction to a better path. These songs teach one not to be hesitant, reluctant, complain, impatient, over-emotional, lazy, and overburdened. Further, it teaches one to prepare for challenges, be physically and mentally fit, be self-aware, protect, respect the sacred, and never accept defeat. Navajo men and women today have no concept of the Protection Way; therefore, there is much divisiveness between citizens. This round is also to introduce hunting skills. Initially, the bow and arrow are considered as *Jish* (Medicine Bundle) and used only to hunt deer, elk, bear, mountain sheep, mountain lion, and bobcats, where parts of the animals can help heal humans during a ceremony. Only the deer and elk can be for food—the story of the Bow Guard and its meaning and representation represents the weapons obtained from the Giant slain by the Twin Warriors. The black leather represents *Béésh Diłhił;* turquoise represents *Béésh Dootłizh* and *Béésh łitsoh*, and silver represents *Béésh ługai*. Necessarily, elements of the Bow Guard include its songs and prayers. When one knows these songs, one has the powers of the Twin Warriors' characteristics and armor of defense and should be worn daily.

Lastly, I explained how the fourth round intends to establish balance, which usually represents the Blessing Way. Here, songs pertaining to corn, horses/animals, mountains, nature's gentle character (soft rain, no lightning, breeze, and others), Changing Woman, other Holy People, and even the Twin Warriors, the leaders, are acquired. The songs and stories teach respect for nature, care of speech, appreciation, a positive mind, a sense of humor, reverence, motivation, self-identity, caring for others, being true to and accepting one's identity, expressing happiness, being generous, respecting kinship and clan and bloodline, and thinking for one's self. Today, most of our leaders in the Navajo Nation lack these characteristics, causing discouragement, which affects all people's well-being. For an individual to stay focused mentally, physically, and spiritually and make effective decisions for the well-being of all, the Sweat House ceremony must consistently be in practice monthly.

I concluded that such traditional survival skills stemming from *Táchééh* and its intentions according to the rounds and its implications and meanings have continued to teach me the leadership precepts to respect all life. Therefore, my life depends on *Táchééh*, who has carried and continues to carry me through many different journeys thus far and the journey I completed as a doctoral student. *Táchééh* has given me the strength to prepare and face life as it comes and not to become shiftless, to sustain cultural integrity and not sell out to other falsities and beliefs, and to make effective leadership decisions to carry me through old age. Constructing and having my own *Táchééh* has established a sacred place where I can gain a much clearer perspective when learning about one's culture, stories, songs, decision-making, and leadership.

Using an autoethnography method to investigate the problem I identified in my dissertation through self-reflection has also transformed my study and life. In recalling the songs and stories, reflecting on my experience, and attempting to answer my research question, I came to realize how I had not fully grasped, at least not in detail, the valid applicability and potential power of the leadership principles now being conveyed today at the Sweat House. Previous to this autoethnography, I believed so strongly in the Sweat House ceremonies and was so frustrated by the dismissal of them by Navajo leadership and the Navajo Nation government as a whole with various departments that I had taken on an attitude of superiority as relates to my devotion to and practice of Navajo traditional ways and language. Now, looking back on my investigation and reflections have transformed my thinking. I now better understand that, according to the Sweat House teachings, leaders must not see themselves as superior to other humans, nor to other-than-human creatures, even those as small as ants. My investigation inspired me to see myself as constantly learning and that, as a student and an apprentice in learning a Navajo ceremony, I can do much more thinking and storytelling that relates to the Sweat

House Songs about what ways we can live in the world. Moreover, the stories I shared emphasized that our traditions were not taught to us by "superior" humans so much as they come from observing, respectful people who recognized the teachings of the non-human world, which are different when we truly see the natural environment as teachers in the way the origin stories convey.

As an excellent example of the increases in my traditional beliefs about animals and the natural environment as teachers, I think differently now when ants invade my crops, homestead, and Sweat House. It does not mean I may not take action against them, but I can do so with a new level of respect, as I was taught to do when I take a deer or elk for food. Can I learn patience or another virtue and practice it when such happens? I believe my dissertation helped me answer this with "yes." As I went through the editing process of having my dissertation published, I read what I have written and researched, I realized how easy it is to lose the real-life applications of the stories my *Cheii* wanted me to understand. How does ancient wisdom about the different colored ants offer something to those in positions of responsibility within the Navajo Nation that can change the current priorities?

Other new realizations that have come to me during my autoethnography self-study include me seeing that Sweat House teachings do not support the current popular solutions to our problems in the Navajo Nation. For example, it does little good to continue to receive more monies from the federal government and continue building and creating more hospitals, mental institutions, homeless shelters, nursing homes for the Elders, adoption shelters for Navajo children, or battered women shelters without embracing our traditional ways in the Navajo Nation. In fact, considering the dependency on the federal government and Western ideas and unnecessarily extracting materials from Mother Earth, we may ultimately cause more harm than good. I suggested, why not build Sweat Houses throughout the Navajo Nation that can heal and solve problems? The Sweat House is a place-based environment where leaders can learn to respect All Life (wanted or unwanted), Elders, children, women, Mother Earth,

Cosmos, and, most importantly, themselves. All life-considered sacred stories our Elders revealed during the Sweat House Ceremony were given to us by the Holy People. It is our job as Navajo to protect it. As true leaders, we help people develop just as we develop an infant until they learn to protect their mental state of mind. According to the stories and songs I have shared in my dissertation, leadership is about how we walk in the world to ensure we remain in harmony with all relations for the well-being of all. During my dissertation journey, I learned how to walk more in connection with others than I had done before this journey.

Data Generated as Relates to Problem

In my dissertation, I have shown how our identity and leadership roles as *Nihokáá Diyin Dine'é*, men and women, are clearly defined at *Táchééh* and play an influential role in life that can prevent such harmful acts mentioned. Further guiding our people toward a more sacred view of self, others, life, ecological sustainability, and the *Nihookáá Diyin Dine'é* way of living it; with this guidance, when learned and internalized, such harmful acts could then be eliminated. I gave examples of how I used epic stories of the twin brothers, *Naayéé' Neizghání* (Killer of Monsters), *Tóbáyizhchíní* (Born of Water), *'Asdzą́ą́ Nádleehii* (Changing Woman) mother to *Naayéé' Neizghání*, and *Yoołgaii Asdzaan* (White Shell Woman) mother to *Tóbáyizhchíní* are all considered leaders. They are heroes and heroines for protecting our people from harm and danger long ago are still taught today at *Táácheeh*. Characters in Navajo oral traditions of stories I learned about at *Táácheeh* to combat modern-day battles (alcoholism, obesity, sickness, poverty, deceit, and domestic violence) with fearlessness, which serves as a practice embedded in oral traditions.

While conducting research, I knew, for the most part, the consequences of what has led to abandoning our Navajo culture. I knew because I witnessed it first-hand, and the data collected validated my witness. However, according to Western research standards, I had to back my obvious observations with facts and credible sources. For the most part, my literature review generated some disturbing and harmful data, specifically on the consequences of abandoning cultural practices. Of course, as a Navajo man, I could have easily been biased and said that the negative data generated is not happening in the Navajo nation. Further, I can easily omit these disturbing data from my monograph, yet I felt it needed to be shared because, sadly, it is still happening today. We cannot progress until we honestly identify our problems with humility, talk about them, address them, and correct them.

During my literature review research, I found that the abandonment of traditional leadership has led to a loss of language and identity, misguided education, the Navajo Nation making a profit off of traditional Navajo Sweat Houses and other sensitive cultural practices and cultural objects in tourist attractions on the Navajo Nation, the Navajo Nation causing their own suffering, Navajo Nation leaders' disregard for culture, Navajo leaders hiring their friends and relatives rather than qualified applicants, Navajo Nation leaders extracting natural resources from Mother Earth thereby desecrating Her, Navajo Nation not teaching their children about their identity, roles, and responsibility to culture, Navajo engulfed in unhealthy practices, Navajo Nation leaders using the Navajo peoples monies for outrageous trips to conduct meetings to far away places, especially Las Vegas, Nevada during the Professional Bull Riders event, the Indian National Finals Rodeo, and the National Finals Rodeo, to name few but many lavishing trips at the expense of using the Navajo peoples monies. These meetings are scheduled in conjunction with exciting extravaganza events, as mentioned.

Some data generated while conducting my research I want to share below:

• Personal health: According to a 2018 public health assessment of the Navajo Nation, serious health problems, including substance abuse, mental health, and suicide, were among the top concerns. For example, "In 2016, the rate of deaths related to alcohol in Navajo County was four times higher than the rate for Arizona" (Singleton, 2018, p. 4).

• The harmful extraction of resources from Nihoosdzáán Nihimá (Our Mother Earth) (Jalbert, 2012, p. 1).

• Rejecting our Navajo language or using it in disrespectful ways (Allen, 2015, p. 2).
• Navajo profiting from sacred ceremonies (Crank, 2018, p. 2).
• Violence against women (Wilson, 2007, p. 6).
• 77 Navajo Council Delegates and Navajo Nation Vice President charged in slush fund probe (Shebala, 2010).
• 23,000 Navajos, almost one out of every four adult members, list as "problem drinkers" (Donovan, 2017).
• The Navajo Nation Department of Family Services attests to many human trafficking (Gale, 2019, p. 6).
• Native American women still have the highest rates of rape and assault (Gilpin, 2016).
• Suicide is the 7th leading cause of death for Navajo (both genders) at 17.48 per 100,000 (age-adjusted) (https://www.nec.navajo-nsn.gov)
• A massive reduction in Navajo speakers in the Navajo Nation, according to statistics (Denetclaw, 2017).
• Navajo Sweat Lodge Excursion: a profit made by a Navajo family in Kayenta, Arizona, for personal gain at the expense of tourism. Single Day Sweat Lodge Excursion: Round trip transportation from Phoenix, Arizona, hike/meditation in Sedona, and 3-5 rounds of sweat lodge sessions is $300.00 per single reservation. Two-day (overnight) Sweat Lodge Excursion: Sedona Meditation/Hike, Meditation at Grand Canyon, Sweat Lodge, and Guided Tour at Monument Valley are $500.00 per single reservation. (Holt, 2018, pp.4-5)

What I became aware of during my literature review is this: because there is no cultural emphasis embodying core values such as integrity, courage, fear, honor, and tradition, aspiring Navajo people who claim to be leaders today lack a foundation in their character development without the means to become better people and spearhead the problems caused at the hands of our own suffering. One example in particular is the Sweat Lodge Excursion. I asked myself, "Why is the Navajo Nation allowing the Sweat Lodge Excursion to exist?" By allowing the Excursion to continue, we are selling our souls at the expense of tourism, and I can see the negative effects it has on our people. If the Navajo Nation allows this to happen to this day, it is ironic that I was told by the Navajo Nation Human Research Review Board (NNHRRB) not to conduct my research about the Sweat House Leadership. If the NNHRRB read and understood the concept of sustainable development as my grandfather lived it, my study would have been fully supported without many protocols. Leaders within the NNHRRB could have seen my work as dealing with things sensibly and realistically from a place-based or practical perspective rather than theoretical considerations in dealing with problems within the Navajo Nation. Sadly, my experience with the NNHRRB was negative, and I walked away believing that I did not need permission from the NNHRRB to conduct my study because I lived and experienced the Sweat House ceremony and wanted to share my knowledge and experience with the Navajo. The NNHRRB does not own my Navajo language, cultural knowledge, and lived experience rights. Today, I continue to share my Navajo cultural knowledge with everyone who wants to learn about my lived experiences because cultural knowledge must be shared to improve the world. On the other hand, my data also generated positive outcomes on what benefits are available when practicing Sweat House ceremonies that can lead to learning animate leadership characteristics and songs about leadership.

Through narrating the Emanation story, I explained how the subject has matters since the beginning of time regarding decision-making, issues, problems, life's concerns, and how to live life, and I used the origin of the Sweat House and its historical roots to highlight leadership principles briefly. In narrating the events concerning the Sweat House in the Emanation Story, I found that the early stages of the *Táchééh* (Sweat House) were first known as:

- *Hayooł káál Beehooghan* (House Made of White Dawn)
- *Nihodeetł'iizh Beehooghan* (House Made of Blue Day Light)
- *Nihootsooi Beehooghan* (House Made of Yellow Dusk)
- *Cha'hałheeł Beehooghan* (House Made of Darkness)

• *Hooghan Bika'ii* (Male Hogan).

It is essential to understand this because later in the Fourth World, the names of these Hogans were used to construct the *Táchééh* in the form of songs that pertain to leadership. The four sacred mountains also received their names and were appointed as:

1. *Dził Naant'ááh Ła Yilt'é* (First Leadership Mountain)
2. *Dził Naant'ááh Naaki Yilt'é* (Second Leadership Mountain)
3. *Dził Naant'ááh Táá Yilt'é* (Third Leadership Mountain)
4. *Dził Naant'ááh Díí Yilt'é* (Fourth Leadership Mountain)

These mountains served a purpose as songs for leaders with equal capacity and without any hierarchy status. They are also acknowledged as *Naat'ááh Hooghan* (House Leadership). I also explained how leadership emerged from when the four sacred elements assembled and became one, and this process became *Niit'á* (Set in Place). *Niit'á* was then transformed into *Naat'ááh*. This transformation is described in a song of how becoming one whose heart provides leadership for future generations goes through a clockwise cycle of motion. There are six distinct phases within that cycle, and the song below tells us:

1). *Naat'ááh yił yigááł* (One who **walks with** leadership)

2). *Naat'ááh yił diigháág* (One who **begins to walk about** with leadership)

3). *Naat'ááh yił deeyáh* (One who **will go with** leadership)

4). *Naat'ááh yił nídeesdzah* (One who **will return with** leadership)

5). *Naat'ááh yił nádzáh* (One who **returned with** leadership)

6). *Naat'ááh yił nánéézdáh* (One who **established** leadership)

I explained how if our leaders today take notice of these phases, their leadership will have much more effective outcomes. Understanding leadership through songs through the six phases describes Navajo leadership attainment and the principles of leadership are set in motion and given life through action plans. I also gathered some data about leadership in a cultural magazine. Salabye explains in his interview in *Leading the Way: The Wisdom of the Navajo People* magazine that the ants were the first beings to be created as follows:

> Ants came from the Black World. They were the first creatures to come into existence here. Each Ant species had its leaders in charge of the different cardinal directions. The Black Ants (*Wóláchíishzhiin*) were leaders of the East. The Red Ants (*Wóláchíí*) were leaders of the South. The Yellow Ants (*Wóláchííłtsooi*) were leaders of the West. The red Ants with the black head and tails (*Wóláchíí Delchíí'ii*) were leaders of the North. In these four directions, the Ants built their homes with four sides with ladders to their entrances. Our Blessing Way songs refer to the Ant's home in the Black World—*Naat'áádziłgai naaki'ts'áadah ats'os bee danahónaką́* [The 12 feathers that cover the leadership house]. The Ants were the first creatures to come out at the Emergence. This song is the reason we think of them as our first leaders. We say that the Ants walk with leadership: *Naat'ááh yiłdeeyá*. Because it represents leadership, the Ant was the first to sing *Naat'ááh Hooghan Biyin* (Blessing Way Chief Hogan songs). (Salaybe, 2012, p. 2)

I explained that leaders today can use Salabye's story; when put into perspective, Ants established the concept of leadership capacities. There was no leader designated to lead all; instead, they shared leadership responsibilities as they worked in unison to establish a purpose of unity. Salabye further narrated, in the full text of the article, one of the six Blessing Ways leadership songs. The first song sung was a leadership song for the five-fingered people. It was one of the six Blessing Way leadership songs we still sing today. It entails Talking God Hogan songs entitled "I walk with leadership in front of me:"

1. *Shí yishaałgi **Yodí Ałtaas'éí Askii** shitsijį́ naant'agho hadiidlááď* (As I walk about, **Hard Goods Boy** is in charge as he walks in front of me).
2. *Shí yishaałgi **Nitł'iz Ałtaas éí At'ééd** shitsijį́ naant'agho hadiidlááď* (As I walk about **Soft Goods Girl** is in charge as she walks in the back of me).
3. *Shí yishaałgi **Naadą́ą́łgai Ashkii** shitsijį́ naant'agho hadiidlááď* (As

I walk about, **White Corn Boy** is in charge as he walks in front of me).
4. *Shí yishaałgi **Naadą́ą́łtsoi At'ééd** shitsijį naant'agho hadiidlááá* (As I walk about, **Yellow Corn Girl** is in charge as she walks in back of me).
5. *Shí yishaałgi **Tádídíín Ashkii** shitsijį naant'agho hadiidlááá* (As I walk about, **Corn Pollen Boy** is in charge as he walks in front of me).
6. *Shí yishaałgi **Anilt'ánii At'ééd** shitsijį naant'agho hadiidlááá* (As I walk about, **Corn Ripener Girl** is in charge as she walks in back of me).
7. *Shí yishaałgi **Si'ah naagháí Ashkii** shitsijį naant'agho hadiidlááá* (As I walk about, **Long Life Boy** is in charge as he walks in front of me).
8. *Shí yishaałgi **Bik'eh Hózhó At'ééd** shitsijį naant'agho hadiidlááá* (As I walk about, **Happiness Life Girl** is in charge as she walks in back of me).
9. *Shí yishaałgi Bił Ha'azná **Hastoi** shich'į bił hózhó shitsijį naant'agho hadiidlááá* (As I walk about, all the **older men** who came up at Emergence are in charge as they walk in front of me).
10. *Shí yishaałgi Bił Ha'azná **Asdzání** shich'į bił hózhó shitsijį naant'agho hadiidlááá* (As I walk about, all the **older women** who came up at Emergence are in charge as they walk in back of me).
11. *Shí yishaałgi Bił Ha'azná **Tsélkéí** shich'į bił hózhó shitsijį naant'agho hadiidlááá* (As I walk about, all the **young men** who came up at Emergence are in charge as they walk in front of me).
12. *Shí yishaałgi Bił Ha'azná **Ch'ikéí** shich'į bił hózhó shitsijį naant'agho hadiidlááá* (As I walk about, all the **young women** who came up at Emergence are in charge as they walk in back of me).
13. *Shí yishaałgi Bił Ha'azná **Áłchíní** shich'į bił hózhó shitsijį naant'agho hadiidlááá* (As I walk about, all the **children** who came up at Emergence are in charge as they walk in front of me).
14. *Shí yishaałgi Bił Ha'azná **Naat'áanii** shich'į bił hózhó naant'agho hadiidlááá* (As I walk about, all the **leaders** who came up at Emergence are in charge as they walk in back of me). (Salabye, 2012b, pp. 2-3).

Salabye (2012b) went on to say,

> Each of us is like the medicine man, who just takes care of his medicine bundle. The medicine man is not the leader, nor am I the leader. We are both in-between the Holy People, who are the leaders. I am never a leader. The only time I am a leader is when I die. It reminds me to be humble and respect those who came out at the emergence. (Salabye, 2012b, p. 3)

The leadership songs and stories narrated by Salabye above are still sung and used today. One way the song can be helpful when individuals take on a leadership role is that they can be ordained in a formal ceremonial setting through the song to make effective decision-making, including people of all ages. When approached this way, the people in leadership positions will be guided by the ceremony's song(s); they will begin to see value in themselves and others with a sense of purpose.

With the data gathered, I concluded that today's leaders of the Navajo Nation must approach leadership in a spiritual way that includes songs and stories because the lives and future of the people are at stake and must be protected. I also remember my grandfather telling me, "The only way that you will be able to understand leadership is if you are told traditional Navajo stories *Diyin K'eh goo* (Sacred Ways)." These Sacred Ways of traditional Navajo stories are also for all individuals, not just being a leader in the political arena. Suppose we cultivate and restore Navajo leadership to bring back our original power. In that case, I suggest that grandparents and parents use these stories to educate, discipline, and teach their grandchildren and children to respect and honor how they were born into this world. Furthermore, it includes understanding the importance of their Navajo language and identity.

Throughout my dissertation and these pages, I have said that knowing the Navajo language fluently is crucial and necessary for participating in the ceremony. The Sweat House ceremony would not work without our original language, prayers, and songs. If one does not know the Navajo language, one can only know the Navajo culture through English, ultimately losing its intentions, meanings, and values. Nothing holds the original culture in place as does the language. While exploring and documenting my reflections and personal transformation of the Navajo Sweat House practice in ways that describe identity and leadership skills that are vital for the needs of the Navajo Nation, I came to realize more than ever that the loss of one's native tongue can have damaging and harmful effects.

However crucial, loss of language indicates that most Navajo have gone astray from the original sacred path created and intended for us since immemorial to continue the growth process for our future generations. With the many divergent beliefs that have replaced the Navajo Sweat House, the Navajo have lost language, identity, spirituality, education, leadership, and ceremonies. It takes courageous leadership to discuss this problem and the importance of our original sacred path. I have faced many challenges in sharing my courageous position on the effects of language loss and reintroducing our original instructions to the Navajo, who have gone astray and may see no value in our worldview. Further, they are the natural laws of the Holy People, and fluency in our language is necessary for all things in our sacred life path. Language is linked to ceremonies, songs, prayers, stories, and identity to express thought, planning life, spirituality, and many cultural practices that still exist for the Navajo people today that can harmonize potential.

Nevertheless, as a nation, to some degree, the Navajo are not utilizing their language and cultural practices with a sense of urgency and purpose in the context of the home, politics, education, workforce, and life in general. Navajo seem to no longer rely on traditional wisdom and knowledge for effective decision-making or addressing problems in these contexts. Had I not learned to speak the sacred language, I would have never received a traditional education, nor could I carry on conversations and learn the meanings and purpose of ceremonies, songs, prayers, and stories from this authentic worldview of my grandparents.

Utilizing Navajo culture, driven by language, is the sacred path the Holy People intended as the best and most appropriate course of action regarding how the Nation should identify itself with conviction, authority, and power. If my grandparents had not stayed in tune with their Original

Instructions, I would most likely be a lost soul, asking myself questions such as, "Who am I? What is my clan? Who are my Grandparents? Who are my family? Where am I originally from? Why do I live in a city? Why do I not speak my language?" Sadly, all who have to ask these questions are confused about their way of life, thinking, identity, spirit, and soul, which leads to harmful actions. This ancestral knowledge, teachings, language, and identity gives authority and identifies us with our spiritual selves.

Thus, I am responsible for continuing this tradition of our ancestors' language, wisdom, knowledge, and understanding in being faithful to our Original Instructions given to us by the Holy People, still taught today in the Sweat House. As such, I applied them to my Western education and career as an educator despite so much being driven by colonialism. Because of my secure connection and commitment to my language and culture, I view my life experiences as a spiritual phenomenon stemming from the Sweat House, where it can also serve as a tool for success in public school settings in the dominant society.

As I concluded my dissertation, I made some suggestions and recommendations for people to do in order to start coming back to a ceremonial way of life, including explicitly finding ways to participate in the Sweat House, even if they do not speak the native language:

- Return to our original place-based home environment to learn your native language. As you acknowledge and be responsible for your place-based environment, you can reconnect to the land, language, history, and sacred ceremonies, significantly benefiting yourself, your family, your community, and the greater Navajo Nation.
- Once you acknowledge your responsibility, begin overcoming having a feeling of "victimization" that will eliminate all excuses not to learn to speak your native language. My grandfather told me, "Although you do not know the songs now, do your best to sing along, and at some point, you will learn the songs, and you can lead the Sweat House Ceremony someday." So I say, many non-American Indian people are learning to speak American Indian languages; if they can do it, so can you!

• Find a mentor to guide you through constructing your Sweat House. This place-based context will provide an environment where you can learn and speak your language, stories, songs, prayers, and identity. This context will benefit your thinking, plans, life, spirituality, leadership, physicality, and psychological well-being.

• Start sacrificing your time and attend ceremonies, especially the Sweat House ceremony, weekly or monthly to immerse yourself in the language, connectedness, stories, songs, and history. Immersing yourself is crucial for acquiring cultural knowledge from Elders, Medicine Men, and Women.

• To undertake incredibly traditional sacred knowledge and many other cultural aspects, you have a "responsibility" to construct your own Sweat House to be "entitled" to such knowledge.

• Constructing your own Sweat House, you can go to a place-based context (nature) to find clear perspectives to answers to life. The Sweat House will establish your identity, leadership, and survival skills to navigate life as Men and Women of courage.

For future work on the Sweat House, I recommend the following:

• Examining the role of leadership for females stemming from the Sweat House ceremony.

Using the Sweat House to address the detrimental effects of extracting natural resources from Mother Earth.

• The role of warriorhood to self, others, nature, land, and the Nation.

• The Sweat House is a tool for survival skills to sustain self and others and live life to the fullest.

• The Sweat House is a place for planning and interventions to address the psychological and spiritual impact of using traditional medicinal medicine against a pandemic.

• Using the Sweat House to protect, preserve, and promote Navajo cultural wisdom, language, spiritual practice, and ceremonial knowledge for present and future generations.

• How the Sweat House can offer public traditional leadership training, public school education, and public health support through ceremonial interventions, herbal therapies, storytelling, and sharing of cultural knowledge.

These suggestions and recommendations I have briefly highlighted in my dissertation demand much greater elaboration to explore their intentions in more detail. While conducting the final Sweat House ceremony for my project, the suggestions and recommendations listed above were revealed to me as I went through the ceremony's four rounds. Furthermore, in the final round and final story accompanied by a song to bless this project and the people who contributed their knowledge, recommendations, and wisdom, I ended the study with a final Blessing Way song sung in the fourth round of the Sweat House ceremony in saying, "*Dii Bik'eh Naashá*–According to the cosmos and its nature I Walk Through Life."

Specific Outcomes Engendered

Specifically, Navajo Sweat House leadership is intended for males and females in the past times and still today. Both are entitled to Navajo Sweat House leadership training with the same stories, songs, prayers, ceremonies, and outcomes. Some minor differences may exist, but they give equal value to each human and social dimension of leadership. Further, both can be initiated as leaders through ceremonies intended for leadership purposes. My research supports the equal value of leadership and contributes to improvements in human well-being and leadership for all.

Output of knowledge, including old authentic original insights of a Navajo leadership model that has existed since immemorial. My primary objective has been to create new knowledge and improve understanding and use of Navajo traditional leadership. Each step in my research process produced output from the identified problem: Many Navajo leaders have lost their traditional teachings in ways that are stifling efforts for optimal well-being for all. The problem statement led to outputs including improved research methods, data collection and analysis, new knowledge and innovations, self-discoveries, and my recommendations. Further, this can influence changes in Navajo individuals in relearning their identities, language, culture, and traditions. This can influence the Navajo as a society and their government and change policies and practices using traditional Navajo leadership. A system of transformation and better outcomes of prominent leadership having integrity, self-awareness, courage, and gratitude to maximize the success and well-being of all Navajo. Something prominent that can easily be noticed, seen, accessed, and meet the needs of "all" Navajo with longer terms and outcomes for generations.

As I have shared in my open monograph, prominent evidence of my grandfather's leadership is the multiple green pastures secured by miles and miles of stretched fence lines for cattle range management. Other examples of what he built that are still visible today are his traditional Hoogan, his Sweat House, his Corn Field, his home, his work areas, water wells, roads, and trails. These prominent developments are how he defined traditional leadership. They are entities he used during his time, created for his children and us, the grandchildren. He left us important prominent landmark places like his Sweat House to conduct ceremonies for our well-being; a place to plant corn; a place to raise cattle; a place to sweat our bodies to cleanse our minds, body, and spirit; and a place to live with assurance and stability to continue to prosper and carry on the traditions he established. His vision for what he set was thought about, planned, and prayed into existence when he conducted a Sweat House ceremony embedded with many ancient teachings of our ancestors. A few examples of his many prominent leadership still visible today on the homestead he established for "all" to benefit from in many ways. In the same way, our Navajo Nation must do the same now and for the next generation.

About the Author

Dr. Perry R. James (Tábąąhí, Táchii'nii, Áshiihí, and Táneszahnii), traditionalist and fluent speaker of the Nihok'aa Diyin Dine'é Bila' Ashdla'ii (Sacred Five-fingered People of the Earth Surface) of the Navajo tribe from Continental Divide, New Mexico. He is an Assistant Professor of Bilingual Education at Western New Mexico University. His work as a hunter, trail-runner, rancher, warrior (U.S. Army Veteran Paratrooper), cultural relations specialist, educator, researcher, leader, and writer is familiar with ways of knowing in a Navajo traditional Place-based and Worldview context. This familiarity with Place-based and Worldview context creates a sense of sacred place, story/songs, ceremony, history, ecological sustainability, and philosophy essential to the survival of the Nihok'aa Diyin Dine'é Bila' Ashdla'ii. His research interest stems from autoethnography, which addresses the significant need for American Indian scholars to conduct and present research that respects their ways of understanding and reflects how American Indian People wish to be understood.

References

Allen, E. (2015). *Adi Staff Reporter* (2020) Letters: Reasons Why I Did Not Learn Diné Bizaad from https://navajotimes.com/opinion/letters-reasons-why-i-did-not-learn-dine-bizaad/

Clahchischiligi, S. (2020). Perspective: Writer checks in on elders, finds hunger, neglect. Retrieved August 08, 2020, from https://indiancountrytoday.com/news/perspective-writer-checks--in-on-elders-finds-hunger-neglect-0VGKrz7tVUezjScIz6kjeg

Crank, J. (2018). Traditional Navajo Sweat Lodge, Retrieved February 26, 2019, from http://www.quantumnavigation.net/traditional-navajo-sweat-lodge.html.

Denetclaw, P. (2017, November 16). Data shows huge reduction in Diné speakers. *Navajo Times*, p. A2.

Donovan, B. (2017, January 19). 50 years ago: Alcoholism, Litell, and 10,000 Navajos. *Navajo Times*, p. A1.

Gale, E. (2019). Influencing policy solutions: Navajo Nation human trafficking white paper. Retrieved from http://www.tribal-institute.org/2018/B9PP.pdf

Gilpin, L. (2016, June 07). Native American women still have the highest rates of rape and assault. Retrieved September 30, 2020, from https://www.hcn.org/articles/tribal-affairs-why-native-american-women-still-have-the-highest-rates-of-rape-and-assault

Holt, R. (2018). Seed of Life Institute and the SOLI school.www.quantumnavigation.net/traditional-navajo-sweat-lodge.html

Jalbert, K. (2012). http://www.3helix.rpi.edu/?tag=navajo-nation

Locke, K. (2020). Nez-Lizer approve some CARES Act funding, vetoes another $73 million. Retrieved August 13, 2020, from https://www.nhonews.com/

news/2020/jul/14/nez-lizer-approve-some-cares-act-funding-vetoes-an/

Salabye, E. J., Jr. (2012a). Ants in the black world. *Leading the way: The wisdom of the Navajo, 8*(12), 1-24.

Salabye, E. J., Jr. (2012b). A leadership song. *Leading the way: The wisdom of the Navajo, 10*(11), 1-32.

Shebala, M. (2010, October 28). 77 delegates, VP charged in slush fund probe. *Navajo Times*, p. A1.

Singleton, L. (2018, May 30). Substance abuse, mental health, suicide, and poverty top issues. *White Mountain Independent.* https://www.wmicentral.com/news/latest_news/substance-abuse-mental-health-suicide-and-poverty-top-issues/article_a924cd89-b829-5084-b848-b3ac3e94b406.html

CHAPTER 3

SHATTERING THE GLASS CEILING

Cultivating Grit, Growth Mindset, and Self-Efficacy in Pre-Adolescent Elementary Students

Viola Hoskie

The crunch of *shicheii's* boots on fresh fallen snow in the early morning, with the sun rising to the east over the horizon above a hidden oasis we called Sandsprings, came closer to the house. With his coaxing, I walked outside barefoot into the snow. Gentle flurries fluttered to the ground adding yet another layer to the white padding. I quickly scooped up a handful of snow and washed my face, arms, and legs with the snow. I yelled into the morning silence. With teeth chattering and senses fully awake, I ran back inside to stand by the fire crackling in the wood stove to warm up my shivering body. As I grew older, I found myself able to withstand the harsh cold of winter while I carried in wood or walked the mile or so to my grandparents from the bus stop.

Snow bathing is still a tradition carried on by family members. *Shicheii* made his journey a little over three years ago, but his teachings about the importance of snowbathing remain as poignant today as it was when I was just a young girl. I realized the importance of this special once-a-year phenomenon. It was meant not only to prepare me to withstand the harsh winters, but to also build a strong mindset. As I grew older, I challenged myself to bathe in the snow a little longer. When I yelled that morning as a young *Diné* girl, I was developing a strong voice. My teacher's voice used to help young Diné students. This strong mindset has carried me through the tough challenges of being a Diné teenager, through my bachelor's and master's programs, and my doctoral studies.

Shicheii's teachings was the inspiration for my study. I observed my mom and her siblings as they dealt with challenging situations from single parenthood to being a matriarch of a family. My youngest aunt, my uncle, and cousin work tirelessly to carry on my grandparent's ranching and farming. The younger generation completed their college studies despite the statistics that suggested they would not succeed. My brothers, sisters, and cousins follow *shicheii's* mantra of working hard with everything you have. In my own classroom, I saw instances of children rising above complicated situations to be recognized for academic achievements. I often wondered what set them apart from others.

I reflected on my own journey and concluded that it was my own strong will that allowed me to persevere, the very construct *shicheii* stressed to me throughout my life. My grandfather overcame many challenges early in his life, and I believe that was the reason he stressed grit, growth mindset, and self-efficacy. In our family, we followed Navajo traditions such as bathing in the snow to build grit against tough winter conditions, and to know that tough times were temporary. I stood by my grandmother as she prayed to the East in the early mornings. She often asked the deities for a strong mind and healthy body. Upon reflection, having a strong mind was important to my family. It still is and I often pray for a resilient mind. It was not until I began to explore literature, that I learned that my grandparent's teachings are rooted in the Navajo epistemology, *Sa'ah Naaghái Bik'eh Hózhóón* (Nez, 2018).

Grit, growth mindset, and self-efficacy, while explained and widely understood in the context of communities outside of the Navajo Nation, are part of Diné teachings in *Sa'ah Naaghai Bik'eh Hoozhoon.* During the COVID pandemic, former Navajo Nation Vice-Present Rex Lee Jim gave a poignant talk about the Navajo philosophy of walking and praying at dawn. He reinforced the need to put prayers into action. For instance, he shared that running at dawn repeatedly for one year will build physical strength, personal grit, and resilience, which then can be transferred to other parts of a person's life. Benally (1994) added this about *Sa'ah Naaghai Bik'eh Hoozhoon* and learning:

> Each individual is endowed with mental abilities and powers that need guidance and development. A mind is like plants in a field. It must be nourished and tended for it to grow strong. Weeds must be cleared or they will choke the young plants. Navajo pedagogy does not leave the development of the mind to chance. (p. 26)

Lee (2004) said *Sa'ah Naagháí Bik'eh Hózhóón* "is a foundational value that embodies the way Diné people are supposed to live their lives" (p. 1). He further defined SNBH as "long life and happiness" (p. 1). Haskie (2002) described *Sa'ah Naagháí Bik'eh Hózhóón* as balancing the negative and positive forces in life to achieve Hozho. The teachings of SNBH come from the stories of our ancestors with the intent to transfer teachings on how to live a well-balanced and healthy life (Lee, 2004; Haskie, 2002). I came to realize that the teachings of *shicheii* were rooted in *Sa'ah Naagháí Bik'eh Hózhóón* as he reiterated the importance of hard work, mental strength, and resilience. These three components are what grit, growth mindset, and self-efficacy mean to me, and I wish to instill these teachings in my students too.

I was fortunate to have *shicheii, shimasani* and *shi nali asdzaan* be the guiding hands and I wanted to afford those same teachings to my students who may otherwise not have received lessons on grit, growth mindset, and self-efficacy. Benally (1992) emphasized the importance of listening to the teachings of elders, especially when they talk about, "If things are to be, it's up to you" (p. 3). Indigenous wisdom has enabled our grandparents to power through life's challenges, and it can help our students realize the best versions of themselves both academically and emotionally.

Our elders share many teachings on grit, growth mindset, and self-efficacy. I was familiar with typical phrases like *"T'áá hwó' ají t'éego"*. I used Wilson Aronlith's (2017) Diné principles of learning to match the Western understanding of grit, growth mindset, and self-efficacy with

Diné understanding. Grit is *t'áá'oolwolíbee* (use all your strengths and capacities), a growth mindset is *t'aa hó'ajit'éego* (it is up to you), and self-efficacy is *t'aa 'aníįjinízin* (believing in oneself). My goal in conducting this study was to discover whether a well-developed set of interventions teaching grit and growth mindset, driven by a desire to ingrain *t'áá'oolwolíbee, t'aa hó'ajit'éego*, and *t'aa 'aníįjinízin*, would develop self-efficacy in fifth grade students.

My fifth grade students at a public school in northwest New Mexico either ride buses in from neighboring Navajo Nation communities or walk from nearby houses and apartments. Of the thirteen students who participated in the study, 11 were *Diné*, 1 was *Diné* and Hispanic, and 1 was Caucasian. I was fortunate to be with this particular group for two years. We spent their fourth-grade year online during the COVID-19 pandemic and back in the classroom their 5th grade year. As a Title I school, all of the students are afforded free breakfasts and lunches.

Their answers on the student demographics sheet showed they viewed math as their favorite subject. On the other hand, they found reading to be challenging. The students also viewed science and writing as perceived weaknesses. For some of the students, academic performance was not their only struggle. There were socioeconomic factors, the difficulty of living in a single parent home, and trying to understand a parent's struggle with substance abuse. Other challenges included poverty, homelessness, food insecurity, and low self-esteem. This particular group had one another challenge. Just over a fourth had lost a close family member, including a parent, during the pandemic.

Dr. Timothy Benally (2017) reiterated these challenges in his study and added high rates of unemployment and loss of cultural teachings and values. The consequence of having to deal with numerous obstacles can lead to people feeling hopeless. The effects of hopelessness can lead to the inability of students to overcome the glass ceiling (Cohen, 2014). According to Duckworth (2016), increased levels of grit can lead to increased feelings of hope. Navajo children only need to look within themselves as children and grandchildren of the *Diyin Diné'e* and use the teachings of strength and resolve to overcome challenges.

The six-week long study began a month and a half into the new school year. Students took three measurements: an 8-Item Grit Survey for Children (Duckworth & Quinn, 2016), the Implicit Theories of Intelligence Children's Self-Form (Dweck, 1975), and the Self-Efficacy Scale for Children (Bandura, 2006) before and after the focused activities we did in class. They were also interviewed before the study and in an exit interview after.

We spent each morning for the next month learning about grit, growth mindset, and self-efficacy through a plethora of activities beginning with a model of the human brain. The brain is intriguing to students. Student discourse centered around the discussion of the structure. Many noticed the wrinkles and intricate folds within our brain. To approximate the size, we put our fists together. Shimasani would say, "Ni tsiighą́ą́' ba'ahoolya", and in turn I repeated the phrase to my students, "Take care of your brain". We identified a skill, myself included, not yet mastered, and observed how the brain makes connections via neurons and synapses to build understanding. Moose concluded that a person's goal is to build millions and millions of connections through learning. The students marveled at the infinite ability of our brain to hold information.

Together we learned about the journey of the Twin Heroes, *Naayéé'neizghání* (Slayer of Monsters) and *Tóbájíshchíní* (Born for Water), as they faced obstacles on their journey to see their father, the Sun. In a related book, "Race to the Sun" by Rebecca Roanhorse, Nizhoni Begay faces similar trials on a journey to save her father from evil forces. Our class discussions centered around the role of *t'áá'oolwolíbee* (grit) as Nizhoni completed the tasks. Other books we read were "Insignificant Events in the Life of a Cactus" by Dusti Bowling. With a recent group, the class visualized the change Brian Robeson went through as he went from lacking confidence to having a strong mindset in the novel, "Hatchet" by Gary Paulsen.

My students kept a journal, and we called it Our Best Selves notebook. In it, they recorded what they learned about grit, growth mindset, and self-efficacy. Other contents included motivation quotes, personal goals, personal reflections, and lists of positive statements about themselves. In his notebook, Warren reflected, "Having a strong mind that can handle almost anything bad that happens. Your mind doesn't focus on those. They move on to the great things that happen." In a recent journal, Skye sketched a brain with neurons and synapses labeled. She noted her goal was to make her brain as wrinkly as possible by making more connections through learning.

Toward the end of the six week study, it began to flurry outside. The energy level in the classroom amped up. The next morning, students meandered in after a two-hour weather delay. I share my experiences as a young *Diné* girl snow bathing in fresh fallen snow. We made a list of the benefits of snow bathing. Our conclusions included keeping our skin young and smooth, to toughen us up, and to feel energized. Everyone in the study group opted to go outside and wash their face with the snow. Even as we raced back into the classroom to lessen the sting of the coldness, the mood of the classroom was one of accomplishment and strength. I couldn't help but think of memories of my grandpa's encouragement and teachings about snow bathing.

In another activity, each of my students received a mason jar. A supply of slips of paper were available to have students write appositives. Within a week or two, each jar was filled with messages written on brightly colored paper. While they were at PE, I randomly pulled out slips of paper and my heart lightened at the words I saw: *You can do it, You are smart,* and *It will take time but keep trying.* Whenever students felt like they needed a reminder, they pulled a slip from the appositive jar to motivate themselves.

The six weeks went by quickly. In the blink of an eye, the group of thirteen students took the post surveys. My colleague, Kathleen, conducted the post interviews for me. The data showed some unexpected results, perhaps my students' articulation on grit, growth mindset, and self-efficacy having the most substantial change.

On the 8-Item Grit Survey for Children (Duckworth & Quinn, 2016), my students initially averaged a score of 2.46. The post-test score was 2.60.

I used a paired-samples t-Test to analyze the pre-test to post-test data. The effect size was small. However, there were significant changes on several questions. The data revealed more students felt like they could set a goal and pursue it for long periods of time. There was also an increased score on the following statement: "I am diligent (hard working and careful)". The small increase in effect size is understandable. McGlynn and Kelly (2017) concluded that building grit is more of a process lasting a whole school year. Growing up, I did not become gritty instantly, and in fact I am still learning to maintain my perseverance in some instances.

The second research question analyzed the effect of the interventions on the growth mindset of my students. On the pre-test, the students averaged 3.91 on the Implicit Theories of Intelligence Children's Self Form. After the six weeks of interventions, the group averaged 5.05. The higher the score on the survey reveals more of a fixed mindset. The post-test showed improved mindsets that intelligence is malleable with an increased score from 4.38 to 5.31.

The students also took a pre-test and post-test on the Self-Efficacy Scale for Children. The difference between the two tests showed an improvement of 9.89 points. The Self-Efficacy Scale for Children has seven subscales. There were vast improvements in Enlisting Social Resources, Self-Regulating Learning, and Enlisting Parental and Community Support. In fact, students felt more comfortable asking for help with an increased score from 62.69 to 88.27.

Perhaps the most interesting part of the study were the students' pre- and post-conversations about grit, growth mindset, and self-efficacy. In the interview prior to the study, none of the students were able to answer the question, *What does it mean to be gritty?* In fact, Phillip, a twelve-year-old Diné boy, responded, "You have trouble or something." Kate shared that being gritty meant, "You need help with your work." After the study, Lane shared that a gritty person has to be tough and stay focused. Cassandra related her personal experience with reading to being gritty. She told a story about having to read a story and answer questions. She shared that she had to go back into the text many times to look for the answer. She kept at it until she found the right evidence for the answer. Derek elaborated on grit as having "a strong mentality."

The students were better able to talk on the different aspects of having a growth mindset even before the study. Warren described a growth mindset as "Having a strong mind that can handle almost anything bad that happens. Your mind doesn't focus on those. They move on to the great things that happen." Common phrases used in student responses included the words practice and brave to having a growth mindset. Star expounded by saying *practice* makes people better at school and sports. Participants in the study described having a growth mindset using more words and descriptions after participating in the interventions. Moose said, "Growth mindset is when I am able to encourage myself to always do better. If I have a negative mindset, I would just be stuck in the same place. Having a growth mindset helps me learn more and get better at things." This response was similar in depth to other student responses. Other student responses were more specific to learning in the classroom. Sunshine shared, "It means that you believe in yourself. You can figure things out that are challenging like math or reading chapter books."

The importance of *t'aa hó'ajit'éego* (it is up to you) was evident in Phillip, a student with a specific learning disability. At the start of the year, his negative mindset showed in his words, "I can't do it," and in his demeanor. He would loudly sigh and slowly shuffle his way to the group work table for math. Throughout the six weeks, there was growth in both his attitude and the way he spoke about this work. He would still say, "I can't do it," but quickly add "yet". During the exit interview, he shared this about having a growth mindset: "[It means] to have a positive attitude. When something is hard, you say, 'I can do it'." Phillip scored proficient on the New Mexico math assessment at the end of year, and now as an eighth grader at the local middle school, he still finds math to be his strength. Anything is possible with the right mindset.

Aronilth's teachings about the Diné principles of learning says belief in one's ability and having confidence is *t'aa 'aníijinízin*. Before the study, when asked directly, "What does it mean to have self-efficacy?" students were not able to give a response. Some students said self-efficacy is being responsible, while another suggested it meant to have courage and kindness. After the study, Kyle shared that important traits are confidence, patience, being brave, and standing up for oneself. Moose shared a story about playing baseball. He said during a baseball game, "I planned to get on base, so I listened to my coaches. I decided I was going to be confident no matter what, and I believed that I would be able to do it." Derek went in depth about self-efficacy when he shared his experience playing baseball:

> The task I overcame was getting my first hit in baseball. In my first game, I struck out, and that really brought me down because I kept thinking I need to get this hit. I need to help my team. I just kept striking out, and my batting average was going down. I was like, you have to push hard to make sure you meet your goals. I kept telling myself, "Get it done because if you're just going to stand there and worry, then you're not going to get your first hit," so at my next [time] at bat, I came in determined to get my first hit. I knew to push myself so I could get my first hit. I hit on the next pitch and sprinted to first base. I got my first hit. I had to be confident. Having self-efficacy means you have to be confident and know you can accomplish anything.

The students' conversations applied the constructs of grit, growth mindset, and self-efficacy to other aspects of their lives, especially sports. Moose shared a story about how he prepared to run a marathon within one month. He said, "It means to give it your all, like when we did the marathon. Sometimes we were tired, but we kept running, and soon enough, we ran all 26 miles of the marathon." Sunshine and Kyle also metaphorically spoke of grit as "to give it everything you have to finish the race." Likewise, Phillip and Lane both said they needed to be gritty to get through the first couple of weeks of basketball practice. They needed grit to get through the numerous sprints and repeated skill practices. Lane also said, "You have to keep shooting the right way many times so your muscles remember how to shoot the ball right."

Benally's (1994) words resonated with me throughout the study. The development of young brains should not be left up to chance. *Shicheii* knew this and as a result had my brothers, sisters, and siblings partake in practices to help us build the concepts of *t'áá'oolwolíbee, T'áá hwó' ají t'éego* and *t'aa 'anííjinízin*. It began in the springtime. Shicheii knew exactly when to plant corn, squash, and beans. It was a family event. Shicheii asked a clan brother to help plow the fields. With his straw hat protecting him from the glare from Jóhonaa'éí (sun), the seeds in an empty vintage coffee container, his strides quickly took him up and down rows of tilled earth. Soon it was our turn. One by one we took the coffee can, grabbed a few kernels, and ran after the tractor. The heat was unbearable at times, and it was physically demanding, but we pushed through until the cornfield was tilled with rows and rows of an upcoming harvest. I think back to that time and I remember being in awe of my grandpa's pace and his strong will to make sure the fields were planted despite the heat and fatigue. This special time with our *cheii* helped us build our grit and mindset.

Likewise, learning can and should be challenging for students. How do you nurture a strong mindset so students can work through arduous and taxing tasks? During a recent virtual Navajo Nation Day of Prayer: Spiritual Healing in the Times of COVID-19, former Navajo Nation Vice-President Rex Lee Jim gave a poignant talk about the Navajo philosophy of walking and praying at dawn. When I listened to his teachings, it immediately reinforced the Navajo philosophy on grit, growth mindset, and self-efficacy. He suggested that Navajo people should run right after prayer and practice doing that work. Running at dawn repeatedly for one year will build physical strength, personal grit, and resilience. My students used running as a way to build grit and self-efficacy. Before breakfast, they ran two laps around the upper grade field. Some struggled initially, but powered through until one day they were running the quarter mile easily. This practice led them to successfully completing a 26 mile challenge over a month's time. Moose reflected by sharing a story about the marathon. Moose shared a story about how he prepared to run a marathon within one month. He said, "It (grit) means to give it your all, like when we did the marathon. Sometimes we were tired, but we kept running, and soon enough, we ran all 26 miles of the marathon."

Another way to give students an opportunity to build grit, growth mindset, and self-efficacy is through storytelling. *Shicheii* was a great storyteller. My favorite were the coyote stories he only told after the first frost. Often the coyote did not give up on whatever mischievous deed he was up to. My students enjoy stories, too. In the novel, "Race to the Sun", Nizhoni Begay's journey to save her father mimics those of the Navajo Twin Heroes, *Naayéé'neizghání* (Slayer of Monsters) and *Tóbájíshchíní* (Born for Water). Like the Twins, she overcame the canyons that crush, the river reeds that cut, and the sand dunes that swallow.

The cultural significance of storytelling includes the lessons students can learn from these stories, and could be more impactful with elders transferring these stories to the younger generation. Kahn et al. (2016) interviewed 13 Native American elders from various communities to gather personal stories about resilience. During the interviews, the elders also made recommendations for building resilience and grit in Native American youth. The elders suggested sharing stories with the younger generation. Khan et al. reported, They (elders) shared that growing up in challenging conditions, such as poverty, taught them important values of working hard, staying in school despite the odds, getting more education beyond high school, and making sure to work toward getting a good job or career. (p. 6). The purpose of the dialogue between the elders and the youths allowed the elders to transfer culture-based strategies to assist the youth in overcoming hardship in the hope that they would become more resilient.

Throughout the study, I noticed a trend among my students. They began to use positive self-talk in class. Prior to that year, a student gifted me a glass jar filled with motivating quotes. Using this experience, I purchased enough mason jars for everyone and we began filling them with appositives such as "Keep going," "Ask for help," and "Almost . . . back to the drawing board." I remember one specific moment when Star asked if she could get a drink of water because she needed a quick break to regroup before tackling the project of building a model of photosynthesis. I asked her about her thought process, and she said, "I told myself to take a break and get water so I can try again."

Thomaes et al. (2020) defined positive self-talk as "silently saying favorable, encouraging things to oneself" (p. 2211). They distinguished between two types of positive self-talk: ability and effort. When using self-talk, students use words that encourage them to do their best like "I will do my best," or "I will work hard." The researchers studied 212 4th-6th grade students in the Netherlands. As part of their study, the students completed three surveys: Self-Concept in Mathematics, the Scholastic Competence subscale, and the Global Self-Worth subscale. The students completed the first half of a math test. Then, the researchers randomly instructed them to engage in either effort self-talk, ability self-talk, or no self-talk. The students proceeded to complete the math test after receiving instructions on phrases to use. A multiple regression was used to analyze the pre and post data. Thomaes and her colleagues found that students who held negative competence beliefs benefited the most from effort self-talk. Positive self-talk emerged as a theme from the present study. When students participated in the final focus group, they shared the words they used to get through challenging tasks. One that sticks out the most is a statement from Derek. He shared that after striking out twice, he came up to bat again and engaged in positive self-talk. The following are his words: "I kept telling myself, 'Get it done because if you're just going to stand there and worry, then you're not going to get your first hit,' so at my next [time] at bat, I came in determined to get my first hit."

Amazingly, he did get his first hit the next time he was bat. The power of positive self-talk added to his agency and resolve.

Finally, during the study I realized the power of words. Honorable Rex Lee Jim reiterated the sanctity of words. *Shinálí asdzą́ą́* was always so kind with her words. She also used her sense of humor to lighten what may have otherwise been devastating to me as a beginning chef. Cooking with *Shinálí asdzą́ą́* (my paternal grandmother) was always interesting. Once, I allowed a pan of potatoes to slide off the stove, and she laughed about it. She asked me to try again a few days later, and in the process taught me to look at mistakes as an opportunity to try again. Shimasani (my maternal grandmother) had a lot of faith in me. I often translated for her at a young age, and in my teen years, I became her chauffeur. Sometimes our destination was a huge city, but her belief in me led to an increase in my self-efficacy and that mistakes are part of learning.

Werito and Vallejo (2020) retold the story of how Coyote intervened when the First People were arguing about who should teach the children. He offered to take the children. When they returned, they exhibited the undesirable traits associated with Coyote, including being undisciplined. The people realized they needed to teach the children themselves. Werito and Vallejo stated the moral as this: "It is up to the Diné parents, educators, and community members to take responsibility for their own children and their learning" (p. 192).

Conclusion

The goal of *Sa'ah Naagháí Bik'eh Hózhóón* is for people to realize they are "a Holy Earth Surface Being living in beauty and harmony" (Nez, 2018, p. 17). In a traditional Diné home, teachings such as snow bathing and herding sheep during hot summer days and cold winters enable individuals to realize their potential by knowing they can overcome any type of challenges that come their way.

Shicheii (my maternal grandfather) armed me with his words and encouragement. When he was home from the railroad, he requested a summary of my experiences at school. When he was pleased with the news of my achievements, he nodded and said, *"Nizhoni Shistoi. Awolibee anit'i. Yeego naalniish"* (Keep going with everything you have, and work hard). As a result of his encouraging words, I overcame common childhood challenges faced by *Diné* children even today. I often wondered how I was able to thrive. I attribute it to the teachings about grit, growth mindset, and self-efficacy instilled in me by my grandparents, especially *Shicheii.*

In this study, I investigated whether a six-week intervention would improve students' self-perceptions of grit, growth mindset, and self-efficacy. During the six-week intervention, the students watched presentations; analyzed characters' resolve in children's literature (including Native American characters); studied the brain and its ability to grow with knowledge; filled a jar with positive words they heard; listened to personal stories about grit, growth mindset, and self-efficacy; and discussed and celebrated when students demonstrated grit, growth mindset, and self-efficacy in the classroom. The results showed that the students grew significantly from the pre-test to the post-test on the Implicit Theories of Intelligence Children's Self-Form (Dweck, 1975) and the Self-Efficacy Scale for Children (Bandura, 2006). The students also showed a small amount of growth on the 8-Item Grit Scale for Children (Duckworth et al., 2007; Duckworth & Quinn, 2009).

In addition to improving their knowledge of the three constructs, students were able to talk about having a growth mindset and its impact on them in the areas of academics and sports. They shared vignettes of how they overcame challenges by using the language of grit, growth mindset, and self-efficacy. A major theme positive self-talk emerged, as many used self-talk to sustain *"Hadziil Azh'dolzin"* (strength and resilience). Werito and Vallejo (2020) shared Wilson Aronilth's (2017) Diné principles of learning aligned with Sa'ah Naaghai Bik'eh Hoozhoon. Aronilth shared the following teachings:

1. *Doo hwil hoyee'da* (Don't be lazy) because fear contributes to "self-doubt, self-pity, and laziness" (p. 193). Instead, a person should undertake any challenges with courage.
2. *T'áá'oolwolíbee* (Use all of your strengths and capacities). Aronilth said that building the capacity to understand one's strengths and capabilities at a young age allows a person to achieve anything they set their mind to.
3. *T'aa hó'ajit'éego* (It's up to you) means, "Everything you need to know and want to learn is already within you" (p. 194). It is up to people to believe in themselves and go through the learning processes that will help them succeed.
4. *T'aa 'aníijinízin* (Believe in what you are doing) relates to both

growth mindset and self-efficacy. Hope, faith, and belief in self-lead to the realization and fulfillment of one's dreams.

By giving students the opportunity to learn about grit, growth mindset, and self-efficacy by intertwining an indigenous understanding and literature from successful curriculums and interventions, educators, coaches, parents, and researchers have the ability to equip their students with a stronger understanding of their abilities based on grit, growth mindset, and self-efficacy.

About the Author

Viola J. Hoskie is a Navajo educator from northwest New Mexico. She is of the Haltsooí Dine'é (Meadow People clan) and born for the Tsi'naajinii (Black Streak Wood) people. Her grandparents are of the Bit'ahnii (Folded Arms) clan and the Kinyaa'áanii (Towering House) clan. She comes from Manuelito (Kin Hozhoni), New Mexico. Viola is a recipient of the 2016 New Mexico Golden Apple teaching award. As an educator for over 20 years, Viola has taught upper elementary students at an elementary public school that is near and dear to her heart. She is passionate about developing the whole child by using the teachings of her grandparents. They stressed the importance of having a strong mindset to overcome challenges. Viola believes having a growth mindset can be impactful in the lives of students. After completing her Bachelors and Masters in Elementary Education from the University of New Mexico, she received a Doctorate Degree in Leadership for Change from Fielding Graduate University. Her dissertation titled *Shattering the Glass Ceiling: Cultivating Grit, Growth Mindset, and Self-Efficacy in Preadolescent Students* was inspired by the resilience and mental strength of her *cheii*, Kee Ellison and the nurturing love of her *masaní*, Dolly Ellison, and *nalí asdzaan*, Bah Hoskie.

References

Aronilth, W., Jr. (2017). *Traditional Perspectives on Navajo Language.* Paper presented at the Navajo Language Revitalization Summit, May 22–23, Tsaile, AZ.

Bandura, A. (2006). Guide for constructing self-efficacy scales. *Self-efficacy Beliefs of Adolescents,* 5, 307–337.

Benally, H. J. (1992). Spiritual knowledge for a secular society: Traditional Navajo spirituality offers lessons for the nation. *Tribal College*, III(4), 19.

Benally, H. J. (1994). Navajo philosophy of learning and pedagogy. *Journal of Navajo Education,* 12(1), 23-31.

Benally, T. (2017). Toward true educational sovereignty for the Navajo Nation: Structure, politics, curriculum, and quality (Publication No. 10255095) [Doctoral dissertation, Fielding Graduate University]. *ProQuest Dissertations & Theses Global.*

Bowling, D. (2017). *Insignificant events in the life of a cactus.* Union Square Kids.

Cohen, E. R. (2014). An appreciative inquiry study of successful Navajo high school students on the Navajo Nation (Publication No. 3670685). [Doctoral dissertation, Ohio State University] *ProQuest Dissertations; Theses Global.*

Duckworth, A. (2016). *Grit: The power of passion and perseverance.* Scribner/ Simon & Schuster.

Duckworth, A. L., & Quinn, P. D. (2009). Development and validation of the short grit scale (grit-S). *Journal of Personality Assessment*, 91(2), 166-174. https://doi.org/10.1080/00223890802634290

Dweck, C. S. (1975). The role of expectations and attributions in the alleviation of learned helplessness. *Journal of Personality and Social Psychology,* 31, 674-685. Doi:10.1037/h0077149

Haskie, M. J. (2002). Preserving a culture: Practicing the Navajo principles of hózhǫ́ dóó K'e (Publication No. 3077247) [Doctoral dissertation, Fielding Graduate Institute]. *ProQuest Dissertations and Theses Global.*

Kahn-John (Diné), M., & Koithan, M. (2015). Living in health, harmony, and beauty: The Diné (Navajo) hózhó wellness philosophy. *Global Advances in Health and Medicine,* 4(3), 24-30. https://doi.org/10.7453/gahmj.2015.044

Lee, L. L. (2004). 21st century Diné cultural identity: Defining and practicing sa'ah naagháí bik'eh hózhóón. *American Quarterly*, 56(4), 1159.

McGlynn, K., & Kelly, J. (2017). Breaking the cycle: Thoughts about building grit in the classroom. *Science Scope*, 41(1), 24-27.

Nez, V. (2018). Diné epistemology: *Sa'ah naagháí bik'eh hózhóón* teachings (Order No. 10823922). *ProQuest Dissertations & Theses Global.*

Roanhorse, R. (2020). *Race to the sun.* Disney/Hyperion.

Thomaes, S., Tjaarda, I., Brummelman, E., Sedikides, C., Thomaes, L., & Social and personality development: A transactional approach. (2020). Effort self-talk benefits the mathematics performance of children with negative competence beliefs. *Child Development*, 91(6), 2211-2220. https://doi.org/10.1111/cdev.13347

Vallejo, P., & Werito, V. (Eds.). (2022). Transforming Diné Education: Innovations in Pedagogy and Practice. *University of Arizona Press*. https://doi.org/10.2307/j.ctv2c3k1c4

Chapter 4

Navajo Numbers: Nóomba 'Ákwííigíí, Holy Air

Henry Fowler

At the time, I was somewhere around eight years old, and I remember that it was quite early in the morning. I am roused from my sleep by the scent of my mother's freshly cooked tortilla bread and potatoes that are boiling. It was she who established the tone of the family. The unrivaled stillness of her voice exemplifies the phrase that her ancestors lived by. She taught us to get up before the dawn, to massage the hopeful early morning light into our bodies, to awaken our aware brains, and to visualize the purpose and goals that we want to achieve in our lives. This instruction was similar to what her predecessors had given us. The first light of the day is a metaphor for reflection. The world was formed by the Creator by the use of his own thinking, which is the source of thought. In the darkness of Ni'hodiłhił, the Holy Air Spirited Niłch'í Diyinii Yah'ałnii'neeyání is said to have been the source of life, as said by my mother, who is of the traditional Navajo tribe, Sally Fowler. Ni'hodiłhił is the stage of existence that is beginning to emerge. Darkness is obscured in the Ni'hodiłhił, which is characterized by the presence of hot gas, foggy material, mist, and wetness that are produced by the atmosphere of space. Niłch'í Diyinii Yah'ałnii'neeyání is identified as the supreme Holy Being, the Divine Holy Air, and the being who is responsible for the creation of all living things.

Yah'ałnii'neeyání is the name given to the wind that is considered sacred. The sacred wind, which is represented by the holy air in motion, possesses the power of the Holy Being's Spirit, which is inherent in the wind. Both the Holy Being's spirit and the sanctified Crystal Air moved together, and the Holy Being's spirit is pure in its form. This is how everything manifests and comes into being in a sacred manner to give origin to life. The Holy Being used its intellect to move all of the spirits, and this is how everything gets brought into existence.

In addition to being composed of a male and a female energy spirit form, the Crystal Air was a manifestation of the Holy Divine Spirit of Sa'ah Naaghái Bik'eh Hózhóón. The mind and spirit were the sources of energy that fueled Sa'ah Naaghái's power of energy. In contrast to Sa'ah Naaghái, who embodied the masculine form of the energy spirit, Bik'eh Hózhóón was a good fit for the role of the feminine energy spirit. Because of the defects in the pattern's cyclical flow, Sa'ah Naaghái will eventually expand past them. The Bik'eh Hózhóón is in accord with beauty and harmony, and it also provides protection from imperfection. It clings to the intuition of creativity of the spirit of thinking and motion, and it is in harmony with perfection.

The inner core form of Sa'ah must undergo expansion, maturation, and growth in order for it to be able to benefit from the sustenance that is provided by the environment around it. Sa'ah is a fundamental component of all living things. The creative process that resulted from the organically occurring transformative properties of organisms was the source of life being perceived.

A process or regular pattern of change that occurs as a result of interdependence and cyclical interconnection is said to be described by the term "naaghái." It is true that every reality in the universe possesses its own unique energy, intellect, and procedures of nature. The reference to the natural process is one that moves and exists in accordance with its own intrinsic spiral movement.

The Sa'ah and Naaghái paradigm views the relationship as a holistic system, with its developmental stages being viewed as integral aspects of the whole rather than as distinct components. This is in

contrast to the standard paradigm, which views the relationship as a discrete component. Holistic thinking is an essential component of ecological phenomena, and it extends into the cyclical natural orders that exist in the environment.
Using Bik'eh Hózhóón, all of the components of the delicate, imbalanced movement defect that have the potential to disrupt an interconnected connection system are brought into harmony and balanced equilibrium. An energy or condition of Hózhó is formed when natural orderliness preserves balance and restores beauty while simultaneously ensuring that everything is in equilibrium. In order to achieve equilibrium, it is necessary to establish boundaries, to foster growth, and to ensure that all of the components are in harmony with one another to make a whole. In this way, all energy and matter are said it reach the state of being Sa'ah Naaghái Bik'eh Hózhóón. (S. Fowler, Navajo Nation, lived in Tonalea, Arizona, personal communication, May 13, 2021).

My mother would echo her talk or prayer in the morning to the Devine Holy Beings and conclude her prayer and say, now I am Sa'ah Naaghái Bik'eh Hózhóón. Sa'ah Naaghái Bik'eh Hózhóón is the fundamental path to an excellent, suitable living for all organic matters and life. Sa'ah Naaghái Bik'eh lives in all living forms by the notation of Iłchi'nasłá, which means all form has a good side and a wrong side or are symbolic of codes of order cyclical directions integrated with colors and conform of female and male forms. Iłchi'nasłá implies a continuum of opposite sides; energy is intertwined and counteracts to sustain the system or condition to move in the continuum of balance. As the system moves in balance, the four directions illuminate the awakening of consciousness that forms the basis of Navajo Philosophy.

Navajo Paradigm

The moving action imbues the four air directions and stretches to six divine airs. The four bases of divine air are associated with the four seasons, four cardinal directions, four primary lunar moon phases, and four parts of the day, which are associated with the Navajo Paradigm—thinking, planning, life, and reflection/reassurance.

The Navajo Paradigm is a living entity awakening life and cognition to strive with a purpose and reach prosperity or goals. Achieving the outcome reassures an individual well-being, which is aligned with the order of the universe in a balance of harmony. The balance sustains hózhó, which means beauty harmoniously in every direction. In the state of beauty, peace prevails. As a result, beauty is restored to live a whole life with self and the universe, or beauty returns to an orderly state of matters or systematic order of the universe. Reassurance, hope, and harmony return as beings animated in the system where all directions and within is all beauty.

Unrest may return when the systemic of a system encounters unbalance. The unrest can be defined as naayéé'. Neeyéé' is the essence of not stability and the unforeseen presence of unrest and discontent. Naayéé' can refer to or mean the relationship and interdependence of a system is disturbed and named a monster. For example, the bother brings alienation to wellness. The relationship with oneself in a positive matter is being whole, moving forward with strength, and the relationship is strengthened to grow and nourished with an abundance of goodness. The relationship with self-saying talk in hateful or hurtful terms will bring discontent to oneself, which impacts the whole-systemic interdependence of the relationship. The wrong word talk with intention inflicts you and may cause unbalance to your loved ones and afflict the value that sustains the utmost importance to the individual's life. For example, a self-disruption of the wrong word choices could impact your land, animals, children, corn field, and family members. Also, Naayéé's monster is an imperfection of shortcoming existence that hinders your mind, school, performance, decisions, and life in general. Hózhó and Naayéé' are referenced as 'ałch'į'silá meaning the existence toward each other of balance and unbalance in the realm of positive energy and negative energy or evil and good.

One – Silá

Navajos strive for harmony, which exists in all practical ways of life for them. When cooking, one thinks positively, and the food is permeated with that positive energy. All who eat the food will be in harmony, and the individual's wellness will be solid and sound. The relation with thought plants the stage of interdependency, forming the awakening of the conscious. The conscious is awakened through the sensate of the Universe, which is nurtured by the food eaten. The Universe is awakened with a mind, just like the human. The Universe is embodied with feet, legs, body, mind, mouth, eyes, and hair, just like a human. Moves with these embodied body parts and every other natural order is like the Universe personifying human image. The natural order uses these body parts to see, smell, feel, think, touch, eat, and taste. The natural order is a family of interdependence and extension connections living in harmony, balance, and self-regulation. The natural order itself is the beauty of living and alive. All life is Interdependent, living among each other with its unique energy moving and moving in a direction, arranging its characteristics of interrelated patterns to define its complexities of form or life. The form, substance, and element of life are called silá in Navajo; all lie in living in beauty through connections and relatives. Silá refers to all matter and organisms being interconnected and living placement and interwind, which makes the system a whole.

The Holy Air Spirited Niłch'í Diyinii Yah'ałnii'neeyání with his mind lay the animated form of characteristics of silá. Silá is permeated in the natural processes, codes, doctrines, and existence of Mother Earth (Nahasdzáán) and the Universe (yádiłhił). The Holy Air Spirit, Niłch'í Diyinii Yah'ałnii'neeyání, lay the Universe and Earth and all other elements such as water, air, wind, mountains, sun, light, and all other life such as insects and wildlife. Exist of everything and its doctrines is the metaphor known as silá. Silá is orthodox along the line of this line or known in Navajo as hoodoo, symbolized " – " (Sammie Largo, Navajo Nation, lives in Tsayatoh, New Mexico, personal communication, June 18, 2004). The orthodox connotation along this line is that we are born into this harmonizing and chaotic system. The origin of the Universe started from darkness, changing times, and the order is disturbed, creating the formality of the lie of this line that the Navajo refer to as silá.

Two – Níkíí

Silá is followed by Níkíí conjoined by two-fold of silá. Níkíí is symbolized as ^ . The two-fold represents the human legs. The feet are touching the earth, and the legs are ajar apart, representing stability and resiliency (S. Largo, personal communication, June 18, 2024). The Navajo numbers system is connected and relatively related to the time primordial development of the Universe and earth (S. Fowler, personal communication, April 11, 2017). Silá is the count of one in Navajo, not just related to one object as a quantity but also associated with the connections and interdependent to all life phenomena and the creation of time (S. Largo, personal communication, June 18, 2024, & S. Fowler, personal communication, May 13, 2021). Níkíí, ^, is the quantity count of two objects. The number sense is more than the cardinality set of elements; the number sense is the wholeness of an individual interconnected to the natural orders and phenomena.

The Navajo word for number two, Níkíí, not only represents a numerical concept, but also encapsulates the individual's experiences and senses rooted in their life journey. As S. Largo (personal communication, June 18, 2024) pointed out, the combination of the words silá and níkíí to form lákíí, signifies the teaching of individualism, particularly the interdependent relationship of self-awareness among young people. This teaching, imparted by the elders, instills in the youth an understanding of their emotions, values, and cultural principles, and guides them in building relationships and interactions based on respect for their siblings.

For an example, S. Fowler (personal communication, May 13, 2021) and S. Largo (personal communication, June 18, 2024) stated that a cultural value taught among siblings is for young girls not to wrestle with their brothers or young boys not to wrestle with their sisters.

A. Chase (personal communication, June 19, 2024) showed another form of writing the Navajo word number two, Naakih or Naaki, the standard form of writing numbers in Navajo. However, this symbol, ^, still represents the number two from A. Chase's teaching of Navajo numbers.

Three – Ni'taa'

Capra (1996) describes deep ecology as a paradigm of a holistic view. Deep ecology sees the world not as isolated but as all phenomena of its principles are interconnected and relatively interdependent. Navajo sees the world in this fashion as well. The number three represents the relationship of quantity three objects. Navajo associates the number three as Ni'taa' or Txáa' (see the symbol in the diagram below). Besides three as a number quantity relationship, the symbol with a circle and extension of a line segment below implies the spirit of the human body with a mind to think, plan, live life, and reflect. Capra (1996) defines the values or constellations of practices as the reality of the community and the root of the operations of a community. The Navajo numbers two, níkíí, and three, Ni'taa', teach the Navajo Fundamental Law by joining the last two words of níkíí and ni'taa' as kíítaa'. S. Largo (personal communication, June 18, 2024) explains kíítaa' as the understanding of self and acknowledgment to others or the environment using the Navajo principle K'é. K'é, in general, is the Navajo clan system that brings the kinship a configuration of many clans, which allows social practices of social greeting using the four different clans endowed and inherited at birth. The conformation of the four clans consists first of the clan of the mother, second of the clan of the father, third of the maternal clan, and fourth of the paternal clan.

Navajo is a matrilineal and matrilocal society. The mother's clan is the realm crown of the four clans, which continues to move forward in the generation cycle through her daughter's clan, and the father's first clan will end in the second generation after (S. Fowler, personal communication, May 13, 2021). For example, I am Bitterwater (Tódích'ii'nii) and born for Zuni Edgewater (Nassht'ézhí Táb22hí), and my maternal grandfather is Manygoats (Tł'ízí łání) and paternal grandfather's clan is Red Running into the Water (Táchii'nii). Kíítaa' is now known as k'étah or k'é the social norm greeting in Navajo. Since my first clan is Bitterwater, Bitterwater is associated with my mother's first clan; I will greet all of my mother's sisters and her aunt as my mother or shimá because their clan is Bitterwater, just like my mother. Kinship defines the roles and responsibilities of Navajo and brings forth a sense of belonging and living in organic cultural practices by appropriately expressing how to greet one another. The Navajo number systems are based on the Navajo cultural practices and natural processes of nature (S. Fowler, personal communication, May 13, 2021). Capra (1996) asserts that when the human spirit instinct is tied to a sense of belongingness that comprises a connection to the natural order and cosmos, it is clear that the ecological sense is at its deepest spiritual. Cajete (2000) shares that Native science starts with decoding many layers of meaning encompass in symbols.

Four – D99'

The number system from the standardized math curriculum focuses on counting as a relationship to the number of objects counted. In Navajo, the number system is coded with layers of meaning. Four in Navajo is shown with two lines bisecting each other (see the symbol in the diagram below). The perpendicular bisector is the start of growth using the Navajo Hogan teaching since preconception. It continues in a spiral direction to acquire knowledge and skills and bond with relationships with all the natural order, land, wildlife, teachers, family members, mentors, and friends (S. Fowler, personal communication, May 13, 2021). The symbol for four, the perpendicular bisector, is equated by Navajo elders by crossing their pointer fingers. They rotate their crossed fingers in a circle, they claim, is how the universe and all other energies were formed (S. Fowler, personal communicator, May 13. 2021). Navajo view the universe and earth as alive and living in the essence of the creation of the universe and world. The number four in Navajo also refers to the four seasons, the four sacred Navajo mountains, and the mystic of four infused into parts of the day echoed with prayers and mediated for good health and fortune.

Five - Ish'dla'

The moon is considered as our grandparents. Moon is sacred to the Navajo people. It regulates birth and good blessings to the homestead and wellness. A blessing ceremony is conducted on a waxing crescent. The waxing crescent symbolizes growth and accompanies positive thinking, or a blessing ceremony is conducted for the family, homestead, family animals, land, or to accomplish the purpose of life. S. Fowler et al. (2021) explain that on a waxing crescent, a blessing ceremony is conducted, and the moon phase regulates the prayers. All the prayers become whole on the full moon with new energy, and all is restored with beauty and hope, and you become part of the celestial elements. Navajo call themselves Diné. Five represents the five-fingered people (S. Fowler et al., 2021). According to S. Largo et al. (2024), the number five in Navajo is noted as '(' , representing the moon and the celestial sky. The number five in Navajo is written as Ish'dla' and commonly written as Ashdla'. S. Largo et al. (2024) imply that the notation of five, Ish'dla', conveys the role and responsibility of teaching from the adult female and male or extended relatives. Children are raised conjointly by the parents and the clan members. Cajete (2000) points out that Indigenous people's ways of thinking manifest in an environment that orients their perspective where all things are related and interconnected. The number five teaches the next generation that Indigenous ways of knowing are interconnected to land and the teaching they inherited from their parents or aunts, uncles, and family clan members.

Six - Ha'has't2'

The symbol for six is represented as ha'has't2' (see the symbol in the diagram below); (S. Largo et al., 2024). The number six in Navajo is commonly written as hastx33 or hast33. Six signifies the duality principles as a complement of female and male dualism. Navajo view all life as complementing one another, fostering development, and the life cycle continues with respect to male and female dualism that is exhibited in the network of the natural order. Towards each other, 'ałch'8' silá, using female and male interrelationships, draw upon its energy code that sustains the life cycle, and a network pair exists in all natural phenomena. The phenomena extend into landscape and natural order. Navajo refers to Earth as Mother Earth and the universe as Father Sky; the pair complements in cyclical form, and its system interacts and configures patterns to build a prosperous life for all matters and organisms. The duality exists in the role and responsibilities of a father and mother to teach the child holistically-spiritually anthem to provide a prosperous life for their child in a pattern that supports love, peace, and safety. The parents must live in the convenience of Hózhó. The state of beauty, resonating tranquility of sense, conveys harmony, setting the mind clear and living life to the fullest. Connection with peace in self and the sound and nature's beauty instills calmness, subjected to all beauty around. According to S. Fowler et al. (2021), six represents crossing over from the left five fingers to the next right fingers signifying to adapt to situation by being a great listener.

Seven - Niił'sid'

Seven in Navajo is announced as Niil'sid' (see the symbol in the diagram below); (S. Largo et al., 2024). Often, seven is spelled as tsoosts'id or tsosts'id. Niił'sid' implies the foundation materialized from that a structure is created. From the ground movement exemplifying values, perception, and behavior that deeply permeated into natural order defines the Navajo philosophy and reality of existence connected to all aspects of the universe and Earth. S. Fowler (et al., 2021) claimed just like the rain saturating the Earth's ground deep into the soil, moving the roots of plants and all the soil's organisms, this interrelationship brings harmony and balance to the system. The natural processes of the moist soil, I become one with the process as I breathe the air, rejuvenating my senses as I taste Mother Earth's moisture. This activity is my foundation, and I thank Mother Earth for caring for all life on Earth through its eminent relationship with itself and the universe. Being in the natural process becomes my prayer (S. Fowler et al., 20211). The number seven, Niił'sid, prompts all life that there is a foundation that provides growth and a continuous cycle for life to exist. The Navajo's foundation or philosophy cogitates on the paradigm to think, plan, live the plan, and reflect in a spiral process to fulfill the creativity of the mind, imbued into a relationship with nature that sustains human life in peace and beauty (S. Fowler et al., 2021).

Eight - Bii’

Bii’ is eight in Navajo. Eight is noted with two concaves, shown as two inward curves and connected by a line segment (see the symbol in the diagram below); (S. Largo et al., 2024). Eight is most often noted with the spelling as Tseebíí. Bii’ means inward. S. Largo et al. (2024) conclude that bii’ symbolizes inward self-awareness. Navajo self-awareness clearly defines who they are using the landscape and emergent stories. Navajo refer to themselves as the five-fingered or Earth Surface People and live within the four sacred mountains. The holy mountains are from the east Mount Blanca in Colorado; the west mountain is Mount Taylor near Grant, New Mexico; the west mountain is the San Francisco Peaks near Flagstaff, Arizona, and Mount Hesperus near Durango, Colorado. The sacred mountains are beings who talk and communicate with each other with prayers. The Navajo self-awareness is integrated with the holy mountains, induces fortune of wellness, and provides the needs of the Navajo people. The mountains offer all the resources the Navajo need, such as water, medicinal herbs, spiritual guidance, food, and shelter. The mountains call on the Navajo as their children through a spiritual act to develop social interaction, and right and wrong acts contribute to Navajo relationship and development holistically to appreciate self, family, and the land (S. Fowler et al., 2021).

Nine - Náhas’t’2’

The inquiry—creating a question that initiates an investigation or research—comprises the meaning of the quantity nine. Nine in the ancient practice of the symbol shown with two spirals. Nine is written as Náhas’t’2’, which means to analyze a phenomenon (see the symbol in the diagram below). Frequently, nine is written as Náhást’éé or Náhást’éí in the school setting. You investigate a situation by returning and circling to grasp the meaning of a relationship (S. Largo et al., 2024). The relationship is conceived spiritually, knowing the interrelationship of all forms to understand the context; at a point, listening and observation lead to participating in making meaning of the color of the spectrum that builds the framework to create knowledge inward of your unique spectrum of color that the sunlight sheds light on. S. Fowler et al. (2021) claimed that we reach out to the sun to shed light on an awe moment that inspires us to seek new creative knowledge, and we have that reciprocity of mutual respect for all of the natural order.

Ten - Nééz'lá

The Navajo numbers are conceptualized in relationship to vegetation growth. A plant's growth starts with a seed, and the plant grows out to maturity. The plant develops into the subsequent growth development, and at the end, it grows strong and pollinates and starts the cycle to continue the cycle of species of plant growth. S. Fowler et al. (2021) and S. Largo et al. (2024) describe human development as parallel to the growth of plants. Humans start as infants, young adults, adults, and older adults. Navajo asserts that older adults are wise, resilient, and knowledgeable. Number ten symbolizes older adults who are the family leaders and provide wisdom to young people. In Navajo, ten is recorded with two concaves connected horizontally by a line segment (see the symbol in the diagram below); the two curves joined by a line segment signify older adults connected to the young people where the youth learn from elders. Weaving, traditional songs, prayers, cultural practices, and art are passed on to the next generation so that they can carry the wisdom of the elders. Just like the plant cycle continues, the elder teaching cycle also continues. The Navajo elder's teaching cycle is called the Corn Stalk Philosophy. The corn tassels symbolize that life continues through challenging and pleasant times. The number ten is a stance for a continuous life cycle. The cycle of life is interrelated to all elements and energy. Ten is the basis of counts, and ten cycles to create other counting numbers (S. Fowler et al., 2021). The sacred echo of ten is Nééz'lá (S. Largo et al., 2024). Often, ten is the commonly spoken word for Neeznáá.

Navajo Numbers

D'Ambrosio (2001) asserts mathematics is part of, and embedded in, every culture across the globe. There is a commonality among people in that numbers and their principles are used to strengthen culture and practices. D'Ambrosio (2001) described the discoveries and invention of mathematics as a "mosaic of cultural contributions" (p. 304). Mathematics continues to evolve, and the Navajo numbers perspective is growing. Teaching orally from home is being taken to add the strand of mathematics mosaic, contributing to the global understanding of numbers. The number sense echoed in the traditional Navajo home called a hogan is being shared and echoed like through the canyons and now becomes part of people's homes across the globe. Numbers are quantified, and the quantified amount is conveyed in the Navajo language. In a sense, mathematics is in the Navajo language. For example, Hadishbin quantifies a solid object by saying to fill a container. The quantification is contextualized; in this case, a container could be a tin can, trough, tank, or barrel. Each container presented a tin can trough, tank, or barrel, which was quantified and measured a certain amount in relationship to the size of the solid being referred to. Shaa naajeeh quantifies three or more objects, which means to chase an animate object. For example, chasing three horses or chasing five sheep, the quantity is an abstract count of objects more than three.

According to D'Ambrosio (2001), mathematics and culture are intertwined systematically. D'Ambrosio (2001) postulates that mathematics is systematically interrelated symbols used to convey reasoning to achieve a purpose in life. Navajo have a close relationship with numbers where numbers are coded in nature, and Navajo speak that code. The basis of the number system is counting the new and full moon, which defines their orientation and calendar. The moon phases regulated the purpose of Navajo life and used the lunar phase to calculate time throughout the year. For example, the new moon will rise in the early dawn and set in the evening. Navajo relate mathematics to their body. They use their body to measure and count objects relevant to their daily practices.

Growing up, I played with rocks. I pretended the rocks were my sheep. I created a circular sheep corral from twigs and moved the stones into the twig's sheep corral. I counted the rocks in groups to ensure I had all the stones. I would count the sheep when I had brought the sheep home in the evening. The number sense intertwined creatively while playing, building a relationship with objects and nature. The time I herded the family sheep, my everyday experience connected with mathematics to create patterns that developed my conceptual math understanding. Math is perceiving by handling, feeling, and seeing the objects being counted. Math becomes alive in the movement of one's perception interlock with the natural order.

Figure 1

Navajo Numbers

Numbers	Teaching of Numbers	Word	Symbol	Commonly Written Word	
Ten	Elders teaching	Nééz'lá		Neeznáá	Neeznáá
Nine	Analyze a phenomenon and understand diverse concept	Na'has't2'		Náhást'éé	Náhást'éí
Eight	Self-actualization	Bii'		Tseebíí	Tseebíí
Seven	Diné (Navajo) philosophy	Niił'sid'		Tsosts'id	Tsoosts'id
Six	Father and mother responsibilities	Ha'has't2'		Hastx33	Hast33

Five	Male and female roles	Ish'dla'		Ashdla'	Ashdla'
Four	Diné (Navajo) standards and principles teaching the four directions	Dį́į́'		Dį́į́'	Dį́į́'
Three	The spirit of the human body with a mind to think	Ni'taa'		Txáa'	Táá'
Two	Strength of the footprints and legs	Ní'kíí		Naakih	Naaki
One	Timeline, the past, present, and future	Silá		T'ááłá'í	T'ááłá'í
	(S. Largo, personal communication, June 18, 2024)		(S. Largo, personal communication, June 18, 2024) & A. Chase (personal communication, June 19, 2024)	A. Chase (personal communication, June 19, 2024)	
zero	(A.Chase, personal communication, June 19, 2024) described zero as áden empty, nothing, or none.			Áden	Ádin

Note. The columns containing "Teaching of Numbers" and "Word" are based on personal communications from S. Largo (June 18, 2024) and A. Chase (June 19, 2024). The columns containing "Symbol" and "Commonly Written Word" are based on personal communications from S. Largo (June 18, 2024) and A. Chase (June 19, 2024).

Conclusion

Numbers are genuinely unique to every culture. Navajo utterance of counting and knowledge of numbers is exceptional, specifically related to counting objects and symbolic of each number, teaching harmony, Navajo philosophy, self-identity, duality, Navajo elders, and kinship. Navajo mathematical ideas differ from the Western culture's notation. Mathematical concepts are expressed in Navajo culture, and the context teaches holism relative to peace, beauty, and reflection. Numbers are a spiritual sense to the Navajos because the placement of each number is related in a unique way to the natural order. Numbers are sacred, and the order and patterns are exemplified deep into the ecological network patterns. Through ecologists' patterns, communication is uttered in harmony and speaks symmetry arranged in patterns of specific counts. Ethnomathematics builds relationships with local communities and acknowledges culturally-relevant math education. Math is living and doing it from the cultural perspective, and rich engagement by the culture genuinely sees people solving problems and conveys the message of math in art and their ways of life.

About the Author

Henry H. Fowler is from Tonalea, Arizona. He is a member of the Navajo tribe. He is an associate math professor at Navajo Technical University in Crownpoint, New Mexico. Mr. Fowler is born for Bitter Water and born into the Zuni Edgewater; his maternal grandparents are Many Goats, and his paternal grandparents are Red Running into the Water. Mr. Fowler started his formal education at the age of four at Kaibeto Boarding School in Kaibeto, Arizona. Fowler received his bachelor's degree in mathematics education and master's degree in education from Northern Arizona University in Flagstaff, Arizona, and received his Doctor of Education in Educational Leadership and Change from Fielding Graduate University in Santa Barbara, California. He has been teaching math for over 20 years. Fowler is the co-founder of the Navajo Math Circles. The Navajo Math Circles provides teacher workshops for grades K-12 and works with over 40 mathematicians to promote math education for students from the Navajo Nation. His research interests lie in the area of ethnomathematics. Dr. Fowler is passionate about promoting math literacy and advocating social justice through mathematics. He strongly supports relevant cultural materials to guide instruction.

References

Capra, F. (1996). *The web of life*. New York, NY: Doubleday.

Cajete, G. (2000). *Native Science: Natural laws of interdependence*. Santa Fe, NM: Clear Light Publishers.

D'Ambrosio, Ubiratan. (2001). What is ethnomathematics, and how can it help children in schools? *Teaching Children Mathematics, 6*, 308-310.

CHAPTER 5

NAVAJO TEACHERS WEAVING NAVAJO CULTURE INTO THEIR PEDAGOGY

An Appreciative Inquiry Case Study

Pandora Mike

We all have inspirations that guide our decisions and our lives. One of my most treasured inspirations was the experience of meeting a medicine man who shared his wisdom with me. At the time, I was a regular education teacher-leader piloting a cultural exchange program using technology. Along the way in my educational practice, I had the opportunity to visit with this medicine man. In our conversation about school leadership, he shared a lesson that helped develop my leadership practice today. He shared that he could hear a leader in my voice and in my ideas. He reminded me of my "gifts" to lead my people in a good direction. He chose his words carefully to remind me that education is filled with too many things that distract our true teachings; as a result, our children lose their focus. He went on to share with a strong intent that I need to stay focused on a mission that included "my cause," the purpose of my journey. I thought about my dad's philosophy about the idea that "each child has three teachers," the parents as first teachers, the schoolteachers as second teacher, and the environment as third teacher.

The first time I was inspired by the "three teachers in a child's life" was when I was about 11 years old. I was healing from a traumatic accident that left me home and out of school for a period. My dad was a Kindergarten teacher, and we lived in the school housing where he walked to work daily.

On the morning of returning to school, I remember my dad inviting me to spend a day with him in his classroom instead. I watched him wave the bus to go on without me, and he wiped my tears, telling me, "Things will be ok, shiyazhi (my baby). Life is sacred, and there are lessons to be learned all around us." I don't remember seeing his classroom like the way I did that day, as I had been in it many times before. This day was different, I think, because I was at a crossroads. My dad knew it, even when I didn't at the time. As we walked to his classroom, he told me a story of "three teachers in every child's life." He shared that he and my mother were my first teachers. As he spoke, I remembered that he taught me my clans, how to ride a horse, how to find my way up the mountain, how to shake hands when greeting people, how to pray, how to be helpful, and many more valuable lessons and skills. He then shared that the second teacher in a child's life is the teacher at the school, and the third teacher is the environment to which a child is exposed. By this time, we had reached his classroom, and we started setting things up for his students before the bell rang. I was concerned about how I looked, but I decided this was better than having to face my classmates at school. I was so amazed as I watched my dad teach throughout the day. He read stories and talked in Navajo and English with all the activities. I sat with a group of students in the mini-hoghan that he had built in the classroom, reading, and going over the new letter they were learning that day. I remember that the room was decorated with Navajo letters/words and English letters/words. It included many drawings that he had made of Navajo settings with Navajo children. He laughed with his students often, and I found myself laughing with them, too. At the end of the day, my dad had a talk with me about the day I had experienced with him, about teaching and learning and what it meant to him. He helped me realize that children need to know who they are and where they come from to be successful in life. He always said, "Our goal in life, as Diné, is to live to be 102 years old. Choosing to be happy, using strong skills, and making good choices will help us get there. Our bodies may not feel this way, but we must think this way" (E. H. Mike, personal communication, May 11, 2014).

At the age of eleven, I then decided that I wanted to be a teacher. Like my dad, the medicine man spoke with strong words as he told me that children are born with gifts that help them become skillful and productive people later in life. The medicine man added that our children do not outright tell us, "Hey teacher, get ready, I'm going to show you my gift!" Instead, they show us their gifts at spontaneous and unpredictable moments. So, if we are too busy, too stressed, or too distracted in some way or fashion, we may miss the opportunity to facilitate our children's gifts. Understanding how children have such gifts comes from the wisdom of Navajo culture that the medicine man and my father shared with me. This is why, as an educational leader, I want to do what I can to help ensure that this cultural wisdom is sufficiently and effectively brought into the teaching and learning of Navajo children.

Historically, it has been reported that American Indian students attended boarding schools throughout the United States. However, Benally (2014) reported in his testimony at a national meeting:

> There are a combined total of 38,109 Navajo students in all schools on the Navajo Nation. Based on the most recently available data, 23,056 Navajo students attended public schools on the Navajo Nation, which comprises 60.5% of all students . . . BIE-operated and grant/contract schools collectively educate 39.5% of all Navajo students (Bureau of Indian Education, p. 1).

With the cultural wisdom of Navajo teachers in mind, I conducted a study that explored Navajo teachers' classroom practices as they were incorporating Navajo culture into the classroom. My basic research question was, "In what ways do Navajo teachers weave Navajo culture into their teaching practices to make learning meaningful for Navajo students?" Through the important and useful lived experiences of knowing what the teachers themselves have to say about their practice might the Navajo Nation be able to prevent the loss of their culture and language. I used the term Navajo as a more familiar term for the Diné Nation ethnicity.

Culture is difficult to define because it is everywhere. Some aspects of culture are visible, and some are not. Associate Professor and author, Patricia Marshall (2002), referred to culture as "the consistent ways in which people experience, interpret, and respond to the world around them; it represents the 'ways of being' of a collective population" (p. 8). She discussed the importance of two phenomena that can have an impact on the learning process. The first phenomenon, called *cultural devaluation*, basically refers to the act of devaluing a cultural group. For example, the initial mainstream curriculum found in textbooks on American history did not include American Indian perspectives. As a result, the cultures of the American Indians tend to not be valued as having importance or high status in the larger society. The second phenomenon, called *cultural normalization*, refers to the act of valuing a cultural group in which language and cultural practices are viewed as normal, with equivalent status in the larger society (Marshall, 2002). Additionally, regarding culture James Banks and Cherry McGee Banks (2010) pointed out that,

> American anthropologists developed culture as a social science concept in the early 20th century . . . as an alternative to race as an explanation for why people around the world differed in their actions and beliefs . . . Moreover, these differing learned ways of being human were not inherently superior or inferior to one another–they were just differences. During the last third of the 20th century, the culturally relativist critique of racism got hijacked–distorted by a resurgence in beliefs of superiority and inferiority in ways of being human . . . A broad-ranging review of social science literature in the mid-20th century found more than 250 different uses of the term culture . . . continue to be argued over today without resolution" (Banks & Banks, 2010, p. 35).

For Navajo students, it is important that their experiences in any school setting include an appreciation for their culture, and not be viewed as inferior to the majority culture. For example, teachers need to be mindful of where their students come from and to look beyond the mainstream curriculum to find or develop cultural material for the benefit of their students. It may require teachers to expand their knowledge to learn more about their students outside of school and their families, the community, their learning styles, what their interests are, and the history of the Navajo people. Huffington Post Editor Rebecca Klein (2014) reported that among one of the root causes for low Native American academic achievement is the lack of culturally relevant curriculum and culturally competent staff that understand how to reach Native youth. Experience suggests that incorporating Native languages and culture into academic settings can improve educational engagement and outcomes. Such practices bolster their identity and self-worth of Native youth by respecting the norms and culture of their families and communities ("There Is A Lack Of Culturally Relevant Curriculum For Native Students In Schools," para. 1 & 2). For this study, culture referred to the "patterning of practices of 'being human'—in our routine actions, in our interpretations of meanings in those actions, and in the beliefs that underlie our meaning interpretations" (Banks & McGee Banks, 2010, p. 35). In other words, it structures people's everyday practices, attitudes, beliefs, and language. Culture is constructed and passed on from Navajo elders and used for current situations (Banks & McGee Banks, 2010).

I believe that the findings from this study provide an understanding of how a public school that serves American Indian students uses best practices to promote student success. By taking a deeper look at the teaching practices of Navajo teachers in a public-school setting, I gained an understanding of what guides these high-quality Navajo teachers in their decisions in designing lessons, using pedagogy, and delivering instruction. This study also provided me with the opportunity to examine the evidence as *assets*. The school in this study was doing something right for Navajo students to experience academic success, and I examined the culturally responsive teaching practices that contributed to this positive path. Were the Navajo teachers' teaching concepts and techniques focused on building on strengths (as opposed to focusing on weaknesses) of their students? Author Geneva Gay argued,

Grounding teaching in the notion that success generates success,

> that competence builds confidence, and that regardless of how marginalized or disadvantaged an individual student or ethnic group may be according to external criteria . . . there is some kind of capability within. A key mandate of culturally responsive teaching is accessing this internal strength of ethnically diverse students and communities and using it to improve their personal agency and educational achievement. (Gay, 2013, p. 68).

I believed that framing my study using an Appreciative Inquiry lens helped me identify and describe positive attributes related to Navajo culture incorporated into the teaching practices of Navajo teachers at the selected school. As a critical element of Appreciative Inquiry, I examined the *positive core* that drove the instinctive practices as part of the teaching and learning in the classrooms of these Navajo teachers. The Center for Appreciative Inquiry (2015) stated that, "AI involves, in a central way, the art and practice of asking questions that strengthen a system's capacity to apprehend, anticipate, and heighten positive potential".

All in all, I looked at this school as an organization of teachers having a positive core that incorporates values, best practices, high points, strengths, and collected wisdom that have been working together for student success using Navajo culture. Interview questions focused on all four Appreciative Inquiry phases (AI 4-D) including Discovery, Dream, Design, and Destiny, to identify the positive core experiences and perceptions of the teachers that are related to incorporating Navajo culture into their teaching practices. In the *Discovery* stage, questions focus on collecting information about things that are working well for that topic at hand. For this research study, I asked questions about what teaching practices using Navajo culture worked well for making learning meaningful for Navajo students. Next, in the *Dream* stage, the questions focused on what the Navajo teachers envisioned that they wanted for their future teaching. In the *Design* stage, the questions focused on how to put the ideas from their vision into practice. Finally, in the *Destiny* stage, the questions focused on practical strategies for reaching the vision.

In the findings, four salient themes evolved: 1) Respect for Cultural Values; 2) Respect for Teachings of Elders; 3) Respect for Families and Community; and 4) Belief in the Children. I created this model titled it "The Mike Model: Using a Four D's Lens on Weaving Navajo Culture in the Classroom Model" (Figure 1) to show a simplified design of this study. I chose to use the Navajo basket shown in this model, as the design symbolizes the emergence of the Diné people, the history of the Diné, the sacred mountains, and the rainbows. The four knowledges originated with the creation story of the Diné represented in the center of Navajo basket and now aligned with the four cardinal directions. Just as the coils swirl from the center outward, it represents the life cycle, as does the AI 4-D cycle. And through the interview process, I was able to activate the culture (meaning draw out reflection/discussion on perceptions related to the Diné culture) to evolve the four themes.

Figure 1

The Mike Model

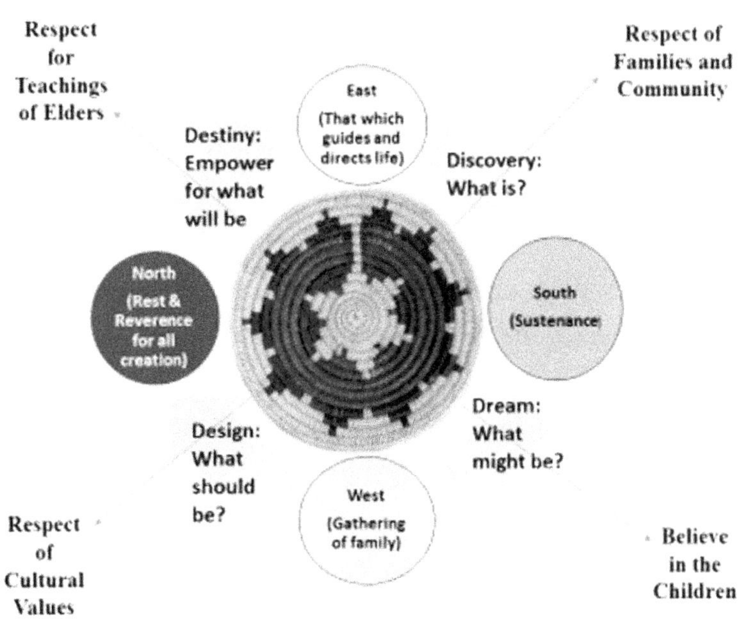

Note. All participants described practices that pointed to incorporating Navajo culture in their teaching practices.

The *Respect for Cultural Values* theme had the strongest responses. Such comments focused on using the Diné language and culture throughout the day and not just during Bilingual language class time. All the teachers made comments about respecting their Diné cultural values in their lessons by using strategies that included a multisensory approach, technology, storytelling, and a focus on developing self-identity and life lessons. A teacher explained that the students start learning about basic counting, colors, and body parts in Navajo. These concepts support the cultural teaching of developing self-identity. Two teachers talked about teaching Navajo concepts through storytelling and learning about themselves by comparing other cultures to Navajos. The regular education teachers also voiced that they fully support the Navajo language teacher by reinforcing cultural concepts by further discussing with their students and asking follow-up questions about to the lessons learned (including vocabulary, stories, songs, etc.). A couple teachers described their roles of modeling for their students to be "language keepers" for the community. Here is a quote from one of the participants: "Well, I believe that this school has a lot of parents that still believe in culture, and I see it, but they expect us Navajo language teachers to teach it. They have gotten away from it, so they're trying to get back to the culture aspects of the school, and through the children, I see and hear a lot of parents come back and say, "My son or daughter did this," or "I'm happy to hear this," or "I think that's what is a valuable part of this school." Additionally, some of the teachers elaborated on weaving Navajo moral values as part of their everyday teachings through experiences done in the classroom or at home. Several teachers emphasized that their students are taught a sense of place to understand their homeland, their clanship, and the importance of learning their Navajo language. For example, one teacher stated,

> They're learning about who their Navajo Nation president is, and they're learning who is the Vice President, and they've seen them at the parade, and we have our map, so they know what a map is and where the Navajo people live. They know that with the Navajo Nation, they know it's not only New Mexico. It is part

> of New Mexico, part of Utah, and part of Arizona. I show them what the Four Corners is and why it is the Four Corners. We did some squares and connected them and said, "See, there is the Four Corners." By now, they show what they really learned. When I ask a question, they will tell me. I am proud to say the children know who their Navajo Nation President and Vice President are and what their roles are.

In another example, one teacher discussed the importance of the children helping their family with the livestock. It was stressed by several teachers that the idea that as part of the culture, learning by doing builds character, as well as developing good relationships with the animals, the land, and their families. It was most gratifying to see that these Navajo teachers viewed these experiences as a celebration of their accomplishments for the Navajo Nation as a whole. As a regular practice, the participants learned new vocabulary for Navajo cultural thematic units related to their home life. In the Dream phase, several teachers made comments that by teaching their students their "Navajo-ness" is normal and by incorporating Navajo cultural moral values into everything they did with their children, they will be a premier school. As related to the Design phase, one teacher stated that learning new Navajo cultural ideas is enjoyable for all the Navajo teachers. Another teacher wanted to learn more about Navajo historical leaders and the Navajo government systems. Another teacher wanted to learn more Navajo language. Several teachers wanted to learn more about their community history and more Indigenous pedagogy from other cultures.

Respect for the Teachings of Elders was another notable theme that was identified with all the teachers. Comments focused on the importance of clanship. The clanship system in the Diné culture is essential to self-identification and building relationships in the community and with the Diné Nation. One teacher made this comment:

> I always ask my mom–she is 80 years old and has a sharp memory–I ask her about students who didn't know their clan, and I'd ask her who I know from their family. She would sit there: "Ei bighan doo

ei nilei ei Tachiini nili" [that household over there are Tachiini in clanship], and she remembers. Another teacher stated: "I guess again, just knowing the family and background of the students I have in my room. We always do this clan chart where we can say, "Oh you're my granddaughter, you're my grandson" and most everyone calls me grandma. There were other comments that made references to talking with elders as a resource and honoring the teachings of relationships and knowing one another for respect. One teacher talked about encouraging students to talk with their grandparents to show respect and work to sustain the Navajo language. One teacher elaborated on teaching students about life lessons using the Navajo concept of duality and self-identity through relevant topics such as home life chores. Grandma used to say, "Ni'we Ni'we! Dooda!" [Leave it alone, leave it alone, No!]. I want to let these kids know that this teacher, here, will say, "Hey, this is what you're supposed to do, and this is how I do it," and "Behave yourself," and "Shake your grandpa's hands," and talk to them in Diné. Another teacher elaborated on making a career change to become a teacher as part of revitalizing the Navajo language and culture to honor the elders.

The theme *Respecting Families and their Communities* highlighted teacher comments that focused on the strength in knowing their students' parents and the honor they have for being a part of the community. One teacher added that a community member even donated his grazing rights so the school could be built at the current location. Another teacher added that sharing and working together is a huge part of the teaching community there at the school. Another teacher mentioned building community using the Diné culture promotes respectful climate of kinship and honors parents and family as part of parent involvement activities. For example, one teacher stated,

I would ask them what kind of Indian they are. They will respond, "We are Diné Indians," and they're identifying themselves as

> that. The extended activity [is] from Diné language class, and I really emphasized it. We color-coded their clan and talked about the group, and each had a different color. I went beyond how the bilingual teacher taught and showed them how they were related and colored them all one color. I said, "Okay, find your relative," and that's how they knew they were related through clanship.

One teacher made a comment about the different views between younger parents and grandparents on children learning their Diné culture and language. With the grandparent's approval, this teacher was able to continue incorporating the cultural activities and language for the children in the quote. Another teacher pointed out that checking for cultural capital is important for understanding where students are coming from. In other words, understanding where the student is coming from in terms of culture, home environment, background knowledge provides an understanding of areas of need in terms of how to use cultural relevancy in the classroom environment.

All the teachers noted the parent-teacher relationship appeared to be a major factor in valuing families and communities. For example, one teacher stated,

> Some of the parents I see during the tutoring say, "Hey, my child was counting," or "My child was singing this song," or "They were talking to their grandma," or small things like that. They picked up things from the school and took them home. It is good to hear the parents' feedback because it shows that the child is willing to take what they learned and show it and share it with Mom and Dad. I tell them to share it with their little brothers and sisters. Ever since I started, I told the parents that my door is always open and told them to be a part of the class and participate.

In the Dream phase, several teachers highlighted that by sharing and helping one another as a teaching community, this led to their national Blue Ribbon award recognition. So, they plan to continue this practice. As related to the Design phase, several teachers wanted to learn more about how to start a parent education program for Diné language and culture.

Lastly, the theme of *Belief in the Students* evolved as the teachers' made statements about building efficacy and self-identity in students through their relationships with them, tailoring their teaching to give students extra support for success, and empowering students to be teachers of the Navajo language and culture to their parents. Their comments conveyed their emotional ties with their students. Here is a direct quote from one of the teachers:

> I would say that, again, when the parents come back and check out their child, they will bring up issues like, "I forgot our clans." The students will tell them, "Oh this is our clan. Hasht['ishnii (Mud), Bit'ahnii (Within His Cover) and Lok'aa' Din4 (Reed People). They're all the same!" They would kind of put those together, and I think that I made a point to this child, and they're sharing it with their parents, and their parents are waking up. The idea of the child becoming the teacher to their parents is a treasure to me because if I can continue that, they can absorb that and carry it with them. They'll continue to learn more in the next grade level and scaffold that. I believe they'll become a good Diné language teacher in the future if they want to be or become a good parent in the Diné sense in teaching our culture.

Because the Diné teachers live in the community and see their students, including their former students, they are able to get student feedback. For example, several teachers stated that students do share how they are successful, at the next level, because of their past learning experiences in my class. That is success for them as teachers. Another teacher emphasized that believing in the students is key to teaching students how to be successful in both worlds, Navajo and Western.

In the *Destiny phase*, the teachers made recommendations for how to reach their vision: Several teachers shared that staying positive in their thoughts would keep them focused. Several others mentioned that they felt appreciated for being asked about what they do as Diné teachers and that now, others are interested in what they are doing to incorporate Navajo culture in their practice. One teacher observed that utilizing the community resources creates a sense of pride in being Navajo. One teacher noted that working together as a team keeps them together as a teaching community. They discussed the importance of staying true to the Navajo culture, to their calling as Navajo teachers, and they talked about focusing on the children.

Overall, these Navajo teachers shared their beliefs, attitudes, and perceptions about their awareness of their own culture, their values about their learning community, and their commitment to the children by adapting to their needs using the Navajo culture. Benally (1987) talked about the importance of using an Indigenous approach to teaching such as the Navajo Philosophy of Learning. According to Benally,

> The theme for a true Navajo education would be the development of the individual through training in the concept of ***Sa'a Naaghaa Bik'eh Hozhoon*** *(SNBH)* and the development of an educational institution that strives to impart a balanced curriculum to its students based upon a philosophy that is uniquely of Indian origin. The proposal that was made over 300 years ago to train the child of the settler according to Indian beliefs and values could finally be realized. To accomplish this it is necessary only to create an educational institution which will place the individual at the focus where the four great branches of Navajo knowledge meet to produce the desired condition, ***hozho***, where one may live in harmony with others in society and in nature (Benally, 1987, p. 7-8).

It is important to note that the loss of culture and language are important challenges facing the Navajo Nation. Professor and author Gloria Ladson-Billings (1995) noted that, "for more than a decade, anthropologists have examined ways that teaching can better match the home and community cultures of students of color who have previously not had academic success in schools" (p. 466). More specifically, the reality for American

Indian people requires Navajos to survive in two worlds: the Navajo Way of Life and Western civilization. A considerable amount of literature has been published on the importance of Native American cultural relevancy and indigenous pedagogy for learning; however, I see a growing need for Appreciative Inquiry studies specific to Navajo education settings. In a recent testimony, Timothy Benally, Acting Superintendent of Navajo Nation Department of Diné Education, shared,

> By integrating and aligning the Navajo Standards with Common Core State Standards, Navajo students will acquire the best of both Western and Navajo education. In addition, students will be learning core academic subjects through relevant content. Using this plan, the Navajo Nation will provide students with Navajo language and culture-based-education, and at the same time provide students with strong academic programs to learn math, science, reading, writing, history, government, and other subjects to the highest degree possible (Benally, 2014).

It is important for teachers to understand better ways to adapt their teaching strategies to fit the cultural learning styles of their students. As educators who serve Navajo children, such discussion themes that are essential for teaching and learning include:

- **Respect for Cultural Values: Diné** traditions, Indigenous identity, Indigenous knowledge, contextual experiences, cultural appropriateness, content, and pedagogy;
- **Respect for Families and Community:** Bridge home and school culture, family life as a resource, background knowledge, parent feedback, "**Diné**-ness" to enhance learning;
- **Respect for the Teachings of Elders:** Family bonding, clanship, story sharing, Community Elders as keepers of specialized cultural knowledge;
- **Belief in the Children:** Positive sense of self, culture serves as a framework for sense making, Culturally Proficient teachers.

The goal of incorporating Navajo culture into teaching practices is: 1) to help children to have an in-depth knowledge of the culture; 2) to help children to appreciate teachings that Elders have passed down through generations; 3) to help children to develop a strong relationship with their families and community; and 4) to help children to know that their teachers believe in them. It is critical that teachers use the Navajo language through the Navajo Philosophy of Learning to sustain the sacred knowledges of SNBH.

Recommendations

This section includes recommendations for policy makers, school district personnel, and those who work with indigenous children. Suggestions for policy makers include reviewing policies and funding to support Indigenous ways of Learning, as well as establishing community forums. It would be beneficial for state and federal policy makers to participate in partnership with Indigenous Nations to review policies and funding to improve alignment to support Indigenous ways of learning. As a result, this would empower teacher preparation programs and teachers in the field to explore culturally relevant teaching ideas. On December 18, 2015, President Obama signed the new Bill titled "Every Student Succeeds Act," which replaced the "No Child Left Behind Act". He said, "With this bill, we reaffirm that fundamentally American ideal—that every child, regardless of race, income, background, the zip code where they live, deserves the chance to make of their lives what they will" (Obama, 2015, para. 17). This law mandates schools to hold students to high standards to prepare them for college and career success. Policy makers could ask, how the ESSA provisions will support Indigenous teaching and learning using cultural relevant schooling and teaching? How will policies change to facilitate best practices that are appropriate for Indigenous children?

Suggestions for school district personnel would be to truly apply the New Mexico Indian Education Act and to review important questions to gain deeper understanding. It would be beneficial for the school districts in New Mexico to ask what this Act means for students. According to the

NMPED Indian Education Division, the purpose of the Indian Education Act is to "ensure equitable and culturally relevant learning environments, educational opportunities and culturally relevant instructional materials for American Indian students enrolled in public schools" (New Mexico Public Education Indian Education Division, 2016, para. 1). Do the district goals, mission, and vision reflect culturally relevant schooling? Are the supportive structures (e.g., professional development, funding, instructional materials, schedule, resources, etc.) appropriate to facilitate culturally relevant teaching practices? How many other teachers use the Navajo culture in their teaching practices? Are these other teachers achieving success with their students like the Navajo teachers in this study? I recommend that school district personnel draw upon these important questions to establish a deeper understanding of how and why other teachers (including non-Navajo teachers) use Navajo culture in their teaching practices.

Lastly, for those who work directly with Indigenous children, I would suggest engaging in dialogue with Elders and tribal leaders, engaging in professional learning communities, incorporating the identified powerful core into their teaching, and establishing standards of practice that nurture indigenous cultures. I propose that learning communities participate in a dialogue with Elders and leaders to explore their own beliefs, attitudes, and values about Indigenous cultures. It is important to focus conversation on the Indigenous ways of life, traditions, and ideas that would involve Elders in the classrooms daily working with children. With tribal leaders present, the Elders and learning communities will be able to have their voices heard on their needs related to cultural relevant schooling. As Professional Learning Communities are a regular practice in schools, I propose that implementing training on culturally relevant pedagogy is important, as it is essential that staff have time to think, reflect, and learn about their own individual cultures, the culture of their school, their students, and the communities of their students and families. Author and consultant Kikanza Nuri-Robins (2012) stated,

> Cultural Proficiency is not a destination but, rather, a way of being. It is an ongoing and unfolding process as you learn about

> yourself, your organization, and the people who work with you. To be culturally proficient doesn't mean you know all there is to know about diversity. It means you have learned how to learn. You have learned how to be a student of culture and a cultural informant to others about the cultural expectations of the environments that you do know well. (Nuri-Robins et al., 2012, p. 97).

Conclusions

In closing, this study provided an opportunity for participants to share their unique ways of teaching on the Navajo Nation. Four findings emerged, as the positive core, from this study: 1) Respect for Cultural Values; 2) Respect for Teachings of Elders; 3) Respect for Families and Community; and 4) Belief in Children. Education for Indigenous peoples has transformed from historical initiatives by the government to dismiss cultural practices, to using a deficit-based perspective in understanding Indian education, to the evolution of an ever-growing culturally relevant schooling approach. I have a dream that one day, all Indian Nations will have premier schools because of incorporating their cultures into schools. In the meantime, Navajo people will continue to experience and practice resilience to sustain their culture and language to meet the unique needs of their children. This research study involved using Appreciative Inquiry (AI) interview questions with seven Navajo teachers in a public school in a rural area on the Navajo Nation. This study focused on the positive core that drove the motivation, the commitment, the love for teaching, and the uniqueness of the teaching practices of these seven participants. By using an AI approach, the Navajo teachers contributed their valuable perceptions about the elements that were critical to Indian education to make learning meaningful for all Indigenous children. Each of these teachers embodied a sense of "Navajo-ness," and they brought their culture into their classrooms. They asserted themselves in multiple ways to empower their students to carry on the traditional knowledges that will shape their future. It is vital for learning communities to establish standards of practice that nurture the Indigenous cultures for the well-being of their students.

About the Author

Dr. Pandora Mike is a Native American (Diné) woman educational leader, mother, grandmother, and member of the Navajo Nation. Her clans are Naakai Diné nili (born of the Mexican People clan), Hooghanlani yashchiin (born for the Many Hogans People clan), Todichi'iinii da bi cheii (Bitter Water People clan of Maternal Grandfather), and Ta'neesdzahnii da bi nali (Tangle People clan of Paternal Grandfather). At Tsé Bit' A'í Middle School (TBAMS), where she serves as principal, Mike's leadership incorporates core values founded in the Diné philosophy to support the needs of the whole child. Mike has contributed leadership and expertise to many efforts beyond TBAMS, including as a former member and chair of the New Mexico Public Education Department Indian Education Advisory Council. Originally from Tse Alnaozti'i' (Sanostee), New Mexico, Mike's 34-year career includes 11 years as an award-winning teacher, 17 years as a principal, and experience as a district director, an assistant superintendent, a deputy superintendent, and an instructor at four colleges. Mike holds a B.S. in Elementary Education, an M.A. in Educational Leadership, and an Ed.D. in Educational Leadership for Change and is an alumnus of the New Mexico Public Education Principals Pursuing Excellence program. In 2023, she was named the National Distinguished Principal for New Mexico (NM) by the National Association Education for Elementary and Middle School Principals. She is the first Indigenous Native American Principal to receive this highest education award for NM, Navajo Nation and the United States of America. She attributes her successes to her late father, Eddie Mike's, teachings and all those she has served.

References

Banks. J., & McGee Banks, C. (2010). Culture in society and in educational practices. In F. Erickson (Ed.), *Multicultural education: Issues and perspectives* (7th ed., pp. 33-56). Hoboken, NJ: John Wiley & Sons.

Benally, H. (1987). Dine bo'ohoo'aah bindii'a': Navajo philosophy of learning. In *Din4 Be'iinl: Journal of Navajo Life, 1*(1), 16-18.

Benally, T. (2014, May 21). Hearing on Indian education ensuring the Bureau of Indian Education has the tools necessary to improve. *Testimony presented before the United States Senate Committee on Indian Affairs.* Retrieved from http://www.indian.senate.gov/sites/default/files/upload/images/5.21.14%20 Testimony%20%20Timothy%20Benally%20%20Navajo%20Nation%20 Department%20of%20Dine'.pdf

Center for Appreciative Inquiry. (2015). *What is appreciative inquiry?* Retrieved from http://www.centerforappreciativeinquiry.net/more-on-ai/what-is-appreciative-inquiry-ai/

Gay, G. (2013). Teaching to and through cultural diversity. Curriculum Inquiry, 43(1), 48-70. Retrieved from *The Ontario Institute for Studies in Education of the University of Toronto.* Malden, Massachusetts. Wiley Periodicals. doi:10.1111/curi.12002

Klein, R. (2014, December 4, Politics page). White House report says that Native American Education is in state of emergency. *Huffington Post News.* Retrieved from http://www.huffingtonpost.com/2014/12/04/native-american-education_n_6264696.html

Ladson-Billings, G. (Fall, 1995). Toward a theory of culturally relevant pedagogy. *American Educational Research Journal, 32*(3), 465-491. Retrieved from http://www.jstor.org/stable/1163320

Marshall, P. L. (2002). *Cultural diversity in our schools.* Belmont, CA. Wadsworth/Thomson Learning.

New Mexico Public Education Department Indian Education Division (2016). *Indian Education Act, 1.* Retrieved from chrome-extension:// efaidnbmnnnibpcajpcglclefindmkaj/https://webnew.ped.state.nm.us/wp-content/uploads/2018/11/NM-Indian-Education-Act.pdf

Nuri-Robins, K. J., Lindsey, D. B., Lindsey, R. B., & Terrell, R. D., & Ochoa, A (Eds.). (2012). *Culturally proficient instruction* (3rd ed.). Thousand Oaks, CA: Corwin.

Obama, Barack. (2015, December 10). Remarks by the President at Every Student Succeeds Act Signing Ceremony. *The White House Office of the Press Secretary.* Retrieved from https://obamawhitehouse.archives.gov/the-press-office/2015/12/10/remarks-president-every-student-succeeds-act-signing-ceremony

CHAPTER 6

ADOONE'É: MOBILE APP PRESERVING NAVAJO LANGUAGE AND CULTURE THROUGH TECHNOLOGY

Miranda Jensen Haskie, Diné College
Albert Leonard Haskie, Nyzhon Studios

The ancestors of Diné people have longed talked about change being a part of life. Technological change is ushering the Diné people into the 21st century. There is also a shift in demographics as more Diné people migrate to urban areas for work. Unlike the migration of only working Navajo males to urban areas solely for work in the 1950s through the early 2000s, more recently entire Navajo families are moving to the cities. Historically, Navajo families stayed home on the reservation while the employed Navajo male left for work a week or weeks at a time only returning on weekends to be with family. According to the 2020 Census, the majority of Diné people were urban. An increasing number of urban Navajos find themselves disconnected from the Diné language and culture. The compelling choice to accept work that supports one's family in urban areas is made while the trade-off is the disconnection from the Diné language and culture. Adoone'é, the mobile app preserving Navajo language and culture through technology, is one way to reconnect the Diné people to their language and culture.

Yá'át'ééh nihik'éí, ádóone'é nishłį́nígíí éíyá Miranda's clans are Áshįįhí (Salt clan) nishłį́, Tł'ízí łání (Many Goats clan) báshíshchíín, Kinłichíinii (Redhouse clan) dashicheii dóó Tódíchíinii (Bitterwater clan) dashinali, akot'éego Diné 'asdzání nishłí. Yá'át'ééh náání, ádóone'é nishłįnígíí éíyá Albert's clans are Áshįįhí (Salt clan) nishłį́, Tó aheedlíinii (Water Flows Together clan) báshíshchíín, Tł'ízí łání (Many Goats clan) dashicheii dóó Kinyaa'áanii (Towering House clan) dashinali, akot'éego Diné tsíłkę́ę́h nishłį́.

Idea of the Adoone'é App

Albert took a computer science course at Diné College in the spring 2021. The idea occurred to him about how to incorporate the Navajo clan system with technology when his instructor Willis Tsosie was going over the topics of (if and else statements) as they learned about coding. So, Albert thought theoretically if he could tell the computer that one clan is related to another clan then surely some sort of algorithm could be constructed based on the Navajo clan system. However, he would not explore this idea further until the summer of 2022.

Albert had the opportunity to attend a summer internship at Indiana University for eight weeks in the summer of 2022. He was surrounded with peers in the discipline of mathematics, engineering, and computer science. They studied under a professor of biostatistics.

Albert's Educational Journey

For three summers during his youth, Albert participated in the Navajo Math Circles at Diné College-Tsaile campus. The Navajo Math Circles program was founded by Dr. Henry Fowler. Dr. Fowler collaborated with national and international university professors in mathematics to offer the eight-week summer program.

Furthermore, as an elementary school student at Tse Ho Tso Diné Bi Olta'(TDB), his Navajo teachers infused Navajo culture with teaching the students math (A. Haskie & M. Haskie, 2021). Albert talked about his love for math that began in the second grade at TDB ((Puati, 2023, 34:34). He had a strong interest in math and recalled being fascinated with math. Prior to TDB, he was enrolled in a Navajo language immersion program at Lukachukai Community School.

The combination of these math experiences infused with Navajo culture prompted Albert to contemplate how he could create a software program that could help the Diné people relearn the Navajo concept of k'é. K'é is a traditional Navajo concept that has been practiced by the Diné people since time immemorial. The Diné people establish and maintain relationship will all (Haskie, M.J., 2023). Hak'ei, one's relatives, include the four clans of how one is clan related. "Therefore, I have numerous relatives outside my nuclear and extended families" (Haskie, 2013, p. 380). "I am constantly aware of my relationship to everything in my environment, not only other Navajo people, but the universe as well" (Haskie, 2013, p. 380).

For months, Albert contemplated ideas about developing the Adoone'é app. He had plenty of design concepts for his app, but realized he needed greater expertise in software engineering. He was an undergraduate at the University of New Mexico majoring in Computer Engineering when the pandemic upended his first year in college. Like many other students, he returned home to Lukachukai as he was thrust into an entirely online education. He was a traditional first-year student in residence at UNM and all of a sudden, he had to transition to a distributed learning model of education like that of Fielding Graduate University.

Albert researched coding bootcamps online. The cost to enroll was prohibitive. Yet, he challenged himself and considered how an educational investment in himself could propel his computer skills to the next level of software application creation, design, and development. His Associate of Science in Mathematics from Diné College along with his 2022 summer internship at Indiana University and all his formative years of math education infused with Navajo culture would enable him to create the Adoone'é app. Albert explained the development of his Adoone'é app at the end of the chapter.

IISHŁA! ("I DID IT!")

Albert spent over eight weeks straight developing his Adoone'é app. He simultaneously completed his bootcamp while applying his newly acquired skills toward his app development. After eight grueling weeks attempting to resolve technical issues with his algorithm to produce the Adoone'é app (see image 1), the algorithm finally worked.

Figure 1

Adoone'é app

Note. Adoone'é website in July, 2023. *(Image by author).*

Albert wanted his app Adoone'é to work on both Android and Apple platforms. He set out to develop the app for Android and completed that app first. Developing the app for Apple took longer to figure out. He could have launched the app only in Android but he held out for the Apple app. Once he figured out the Apple application for his Adoone'é app, he was ready to launch his app on both Android and Apple. Upon configuring the app for each application, he worked with beta testers to debug his app.

Launch Party

Albert, his mother and Lukachukai Chapter Vice President, Connette Blair, coordinated a virtual launch party to unveil his Adoone'é app. It was important for him to launch the app from home in the community of Lukachukai.

Figure 2

Adoone'é app launch and demo

Note. Photo taken July 29, 2023, Lukachukai Chapter House, Lukachukai, AZ. *(Photo by Author).*

Albert developed his app Adoone'é from his home community, so he was insistent on launching his app from home. He reserved the Lukachukai Chapter house for his planned launch party on July 29, 2023 from 10:00 am to 1:00 pm. Family and friends were invited to attend the launch party in person or attend virtually via zoom. He advertised his launch party on his Adoone'é website and social media. At 10:00 am, Albert launched his app virtually and in person. He presented the features of his Adoone'é app.

Teller (2023) who attended the launch party provided commentary on the Adoone'é app "Great app for learning your clans and your kinship to other" Navajos. He continued explaining how the app works, "you can generate how you say kinship terms" using gender and age because in Navajo "kinship terms differ on whether one is older or younger" (Teller, 2023). Comments by viewers to Teller's page included "That's so cool!

This type of information should be available to all of us and it's awesome to see it in a contemporary format for accessibility" (Teller, 2023). Thacker (2024) reminds us how,

> . . . preserving the Navajo language is critical for passing down traditional knowledge, maintaining cultural identity, and fostering communication with Navajo communities. Apps like Adoone'é are still rare, but an essential tool for cultural preservation. (p. 4)

Both Albert and his mother strive to preserve the Navajo language and culture. The Adoone'é app helps them accomplish this goal.

Figure 3

Change Labs Graduates

Note. Albert with fellow Change Labs Graduates, June 17, 2023, Change Labs building, Tuba City, AZ. L-to-R: Albert Leonard Haskie, Valerie Tsosie, Delphina Begay. *(Photo by Author).*

Change Labs Intern

Albert was also a Change Labs intern during the development stages of his app. Change Labs is a Native-led and Native-controlled 501(c)(3) nonprofit organization based on the Navajo Nation. Change labs foster the creation of successful Native American small business that provide a social benefit to tribal communities (Change Labs, 2024). He simultaneously completed the Change Labs Business Incubator internship all the while learning the business aspects as an entrepreneur. Change Labs promotes the development of Native American entrepreneurs.

Albert would frequently engage in conversation with his mother as he considered the Navajo cultural intricacies of his Adoone'é app. Of great importance to him was the development of a user-friendly app that the Diné people could use to establish k'é with one another (Thacker, 2024). One insight he gained following a conversation with his mother was creating an alphabetical listing of each Navajo clan that would be written in Diné bizaad (Navajo language) with English translations next each clan (see Image 2). Recognizing how some Navajos do not speak Diné bizaad let alone read or write it, having the English translations were a key aspect in his Adoone'é app development.

Data on Traffic of Adoone'é Website Visitors

Albert designed a website to coincide the launch of his Adoone'é app. Data compiled about the location of visitors to his website was insightful. Snapshots of data across time were captured to analyze information about who visited his website and where they were from. That data will be presented (A. Haskie, 2023).

Visitors to the website (A. Haskie, 2023) by traffic source included 1,537 from Facebook, 462 from Instagram, 257 who accessed the website directly with 44 from Google; there were 2300 visitors to his website. Visitors to the website by country of origin included 2,288 from the United States, 7 from Canada, and another 15 from other international countries. The website traffic data reported there were 2,136 new visitors. The location of these visitors in the United States were from the following states, 1,025 from Arizona, 379 from New Mexico, 189 from Colorado, 163 from Nevada, 115 from California, 100 from Utah and 68 from Texas. The Navajo Nation is based in the states of Arizona, New Mexico, and Utah. Visitors by cities in the U.S. included 410 from Phoenix, AZ, 143 from Chinle, AZ (Navajo Nation), 44 from Fort Defiance, AZ (Navajo Nation), 42 from Flagstaff, AZ, 39 from Window Rock, AZ (Navajo Nation), 29 from Mesa, AZ and 26 from Chandler, AZ. There have been over 100 downloads of his Adoone'é app.

Opportunities to Premiere the Adoone'é App

Social media followers began posting about his app including Daybreak Warrior. News outlets contacted Albert inviting him for interviews about his Adoone'é app. One interview took place on the podcast, Native Talk with host, Lanasha Puati on August 23, 2023. She spoke with Albert L. Haskie, Diné Software Developer and Founder of Nyzhon Studios: "Ya'at'eeh, Albert L. Haskie yinishye, Lukachukai, Arizona dę́ę́' naashá doo shiyahooa', adoone'é nishłinigíí éíyá Áshįįhí nishłį́ doo Tó aheedliinii bashishchíín, Tł'izíłaní dashichei doo Kinyaa'aanii dashinali, akot'ę́ęgo Diné nishli" (Puati, 2023, 33:06 – 34:05). He greets his audience in the Navajo language telling them his name, the community he is from and where he was raised and provides his Navajo clans: "He is of the Salt clan, born for the Water Flows Together Clan, his maternal grandfather's clan is the Many Goats clan and his paternal grandfather's clan is the Towering House clan. He is majoring in Computer Science."

Albert presented his app at the "Acknowledging Culture in 21st Century Learning" conference by Kéyah Advanced Rural Manufacturing Alliance (KARMA) event at Northern Arizona University on August 26, 2023 (Wittenberg, 2023). He was interviewed during a surprise visit by Navajo Nation President Buu Nygren at Change Labs in Tuba City, AZ on October 18, 2023. Albert walked President Nygren through his Adoone'é app. Change Labs sent reporter, Stacy Thacker (2024), to interview Albert in Lukachukai. Change Labs published the article online on March 26, 2024. Thacker (2024) writes how Albert wanted . . .

> . . .to create an innovative way to blend the Navajo language and cultural teachings with technology. Haskie had to find a way to make it understandable and user friendly, all without training on how to design or program apps. (p. 1)

The Navajo Times reproduced the article and published it on March 28, 2024. The article was reproduced again in the Navajo Hopi Observer on April 2, 2024. Change Labs wanted to share the success of the Navajo entrepreneur, Albert L. Haskie.

Interest In Culture and Technology

Albert has been contacted by several Native American tribes including the Navajo Nation on how to harness computer technology to preserve indigenous language and culture. Undoubtedly, the saying of our Diné ancestors about change being a part of life certainly applies to technology and culture.

His roots combining technology and culture extend back to his ancestor, his great grandfather, Albert Chic Sandoval. Chic Sandoval was a well-known interpreter of the Navajo language in the early 20th century utilizing the tools of his time to preserve the Navajo language (Haskie, 2002). Today, Albert, named after his great grandfather continues the intergenerational journey to preserve the Navajo language and culture (Haskie, M.J. & Haskie, A.L., 2021).

Development of the Adoone'é App

Albert described the development of his Adoone'é app as follows: The development journey I embarked on was intense, starting from a place of no knowledge on app development. My first step in creating the Adoone'é app was to ensure an algorithm could be developed to represent the Navajo clan system. I began this process using basic *if* and *else* statements, recognizing that although the final algorithm would not rely solely on these statements, I needed a starting point to progress. I vividly remember this period, as my thoughts were consumed with code, constantly trying to connect it to the Navajo structure. I had many conversations with my mother discussing the Navajo cultural aspects of my app development. I came away from these discussions with more solid ideas on how to incorporate the Navajo culture. My cultural teachings played a crucial role in ensuring a smooth development process. Often, I would dream of solutions and wake up in the middle of the night to test these ideas. It was a fun and challenging experience, as I was deeply motivated to solve this problem, feeling closer to a solution with each attempt.

After about a month and a half of dedicated problem-solving, I recognized that parts of my code could be simplified using the framework language library. I remember one conversation with my mother about the challenge navigating the Navajo clans and she suggested alphabetizing the Navajo clans by name with English translations. English translations next to the Navajo clans written in the Navajo language would assist users who did not speak the Navajo language. That suggestion made complete sense and would help the user select their Navajo clan. On February 18, 2023, I successfully developed the Navajo Clan system algorithm. This achievement filled me with excitement and a desire to showcase my work. I decided that the Heard Museum Show in Phoenix, Arizona—a show dedicated to Native American artists—would be the perfect venue to demonstrate my algorithm and prove its real-world applicability. The next official step was to create an app on my phone.

I knew I had to start small, so I began by attempting to get a simple app running on my phone. This initial step was crucial to ensure I could code something functional. After one to two days of trial and error, I managed to get a basic tutorial app working on my phone. This app was not the Adoone'é app yet, but it was a necessary starting point. I then began implementing my algorithm into the app. With some more trial and error, I had the app working on my phone within a week, just in time for the Heard Museum Show. I continued testing the app on the drive down, noting bugs and refining it. More conversations with my mother took place helping me refine it. The time limit added pressure, but I wanted to make a strong first impression and demonstrate such an app was possible.

Testing the app in the real world revealed that there was still much work to be done. I aimed to make the app feel robust, so I created a system that allowed users to create a clan profile, preventing the need to enter their clans each time. This was challenging due to limited resources on how to create data usable throughout the application. The real challenge came with ensuring changes to the users' clans were updated throughout the app. Initially, I used a temporary solution where the app would refresh every millisecond, but this slowed the app dramatically. After further development, I found a more efficient solution.

With a robust app in hand, the challenge was to make it work on different devices, specifically Apple devices, as many Navajos use iPhones. Developing for Apple presented a unique set of challenges due to its ecosystem. I needed a Mac to access development tools and an Apple ID to apply for a developer account, among other processes. Once I had everything set up, I began developing the app for iOS using a framework compatible with both Apple and Android devices. However, many systems I created for Android did not translate well to Apple, requiring significant debugging. At one point, I broke the Apple version of my app and feared having to start over. Ingeniously, I created another app with the same name and transferred my code, which worked, much to my relief.

The final step was submitting my application to the App Store and Google Play Store. This process was stressful because if my application didn't pass their tests, it would mean an indefinite period of further development. With a self-imposed deadline for the end of July 2023, I announced progress to my followers, adding pressure to succeed. Apple's strict criteria for app approval were particularly challenging. Initially, the Apple reviewer claimed my app lacked features, but feedback from others confirmed that this app did a lot. I successfully pleaded my case with the reviewer, explaining the app's extensive functionality related to the Navajo clan system. Once I received the approval, it felt like a home run.

Figure 4

Miranda Haskie and Albert Haskie

Note. Photo by Author.

About The Authors

Albert Leonard Haskie is the Software Developer of Adoone'é app and founder of Nyzhon Studios. He is from the community of Lukachukai, AZ on the Navajo Nation. Serving as the lead developer in this project, he has strived to uphold his culture and traditions as a Navajo/Diné. It is his deep-rooted belief that everyone should have access to the resources that preserve and celebrate their Navajo/Diné heritage. He finds great joy in tackling the Navajo/Diné Language and Culture Preservation in the 21st century. With this app, he aims to contribute to his community and empower others to do the same. Together, we can foster a world where Navajo/Diné individuals can achieve fluency in the Navajo/Diné language.

Miranda Jensen Haskie is Professor of Sociology at Diné College in Tsaile,

Arizona, where she has taught for over twenty years. Her commitment to the preservation of Diné language and culture is an enduring aspect of her work, which includes a three-week Navajo Language Immersion project at Diné College, and a six-year Navajo Oral History Project between Diné College and Winona State University. This collaborative undertaking led to the production of twenty-seven living histories of Navajo elders, now archived at the Smithsonian Institute Museum of the American Indian, the libraries of Diné College and Winona State University, and the Navajo Nation Museum. Haskie also values diverse teachings and learning experiences, as demonstrated by the Intercultural Exchange project, in which she co-taught with a colleague from Northampton Community College in Bethlehem, Pennsylvania over a three-year period. Students from Diné College and Northampton traveled to one another's communities to learn, share, and grow in cultural understanding. Most recently, Dr. Haskie began mentoring a cohort of 20 Diné doctoral students working towards their Doctorate of Educational Leadership and Change with the School of Leadership Studies at Fielding Graduate University. Nine (9) Diné students have since completed their doctorate degrees.

References

Change Labs. (2024). https://nativestartup.org.

Haskie, A.L. (2023). *Adoonee Navajo Clans.* https://www.adoonee.com/ .

Haskie, M.J. (2023). Living holistically: Practicing the Navajo principles of hózhǫ́ and k'é. In *Kinship worldview: Indigenous authors going deeper with holistic education.* 3(1). Holistic Education Review (HER).

Haskie, M.J. and Haskie, A.L. (2021). An intergenerational journal preserving the Navajo language. In Haskie, M., Mink, B. & Tiner, K. (Eds.), *The future of Navajo education* (pp. 83-97). Fielding University Press.

Haskie, M. (2013). Teaching sociology at a Tribal College: Navajo philosophy as a pedagogy. *The American Sociologist.* 44(4). (pp.378-384).

Puati, L. (Host). (2023, August 23). Native Talk with Albert Haskie Diné software developer and founder of Nyzhon Studios [Audio podcast]. Apple Podcasts. https://podcasts.apple.com/us/podcast/native-talk-arizona-airdate-08-23-2023/id1518865125?i=1000625497632.

Teller, T. [Daybreak Warrior]. (2023, July 29). *YouTuber Albert Leonard Haskie released a new app available to public today called Adoone'é* [Video]. YouTube. https://www.youtube.com/channel/UCHS5AbSAL_SqDxHitopEwdA/community?lb=UgkxayIshooWNAarSqutOxYTNDooy7AZFC-N

Thacker, S. (2024, March 26). *Leveraging tech to link the next generation to Navajo heritage: Diné entrepreneur uses technology to teach the Navajo clan system.* Change Labs. https://www.nativestartup.org/changemakers/ahaskie (accessed June 3, 2024).

Thacker, S. (2024, March 28). *Leveraging tech to link the next generation to Navajo heritage: Diné entrepreneur uses technology to teach the Navajo clan system.* Navajo Times. https://navajotimes.com/biz/leveraging-tech-to-link-the-next-generation-to-navajo-heritage-dine-entrepreneur-uses-technology-to-teach-the-navajo-clan-system/ (accessed June 3, 2024).

Thacker, S. (2024, April 2). *Leveraging tech to link the next generation to Navajo heritage: Diné entrepreneur uses technology to teach the Navajo clan system.* Navajo-Hopi Observer. https://www.nhonews.com/features/leveraging-tech-to-link-the-next-generation-to-navajo-language-and-culture/article_95d32024-c793-506c-8c9e-f536eeeaa85b.html/ (accessed June 3, 2024).

Wittenberg, A. (2023, Sept. 12). *KARMA event allows educators and families to explore culture with engineering. Navajo-Hopi Observer.* https://www.nhonews.com/features/karma-event-allows-educators-and-families-to-explore-culture-with-engineering/article_f3c43b7f-8313-5b08-926f-f4beb96e9509.html (accessed June 3, 2024).

CHAPTER 7

CREATING POSITIVITY USING HÓZHÓ K'É

Perphelia Fowler

Many Navajo female leaders in today's generation are taking on leadership roles in businesses, educational institutions, and healthcare facilities. As a Navajo female leader, I have always had an interest in the experiences of other Navajo female leaders and how they use K'é. I have wondered how similar our day-to-day lives are at work and home and how we use our Navajo basic principles and values within our communities. Not only did I wonder about the similarities, but I experienced and observed our day-to-day lives at work and home. As I observed our employees and leadership in the workplace, we do not practice nor model the basic principles of positivity and friendly greetings toward one another or toward our daily customers within our communities. Our leaders within the workplace do not properly introduce themselves by indicating where they come from, nor do they share their clans with their employees, and this just creates an unwelcome environment and often the employees feel unappreciated by leadership. If we all greet in a friendly manner using K'e, imagine the positive working relationship where we will be able to see more productivity from employees and are able to build a respectful environment among one another, where we protect our own and empower our own by providing opportunities for growth. The more you empower others, the more respect you receive as a leader.

For home environment, we lack the basic Navajo cultural teaching tools on educating our children on how to greet relatives and family members within our traditional Navajo clan groups. We also lack greeting one another in our own Navajo language. Within my community and homes of my relatives, we mostly call each other by our nick names and do not properly greet one another to our siblings, as my older or younger sister or brother. Most of my siblings call me, "Perphie", which is short for Perphelia. In return, when I see my sister, I would address her in Navajo language, shi'dezhii, (my young sister) and shi'tsili (my young brother). I am the oldest of three sisters and two brothers. My nieces and nephews, also call me, "Perphie" and they don't address me as their mother or auntie (Shima). I address my uncles and auntie as Shi'yazh (uncle) and Shima (Auntie). In meeting with family and relatives, I look for warm greetings and if one greets me in Navajo language as Shi'yazhi or Sha'awee (Baby or my Dear), I will take that to heart, have my highest respect for the individual, and to provide the utmost care and services to him/her. I say this because my paternal and maternal grandparents instilled in me that if you ever get greeted by someone that calls you shi'yazhi or sha'awee, they love you, they care for you, and they want the best for you, and can even discipline you for the right reasons. So, you care for them. This type of greeting is so powerful and emotional for me and to be honest, my late grandparents were the only one that greeted me in this fashion with a warm hug and smile that went a long way. I deeply miss this interaction and do crave this acknowledgement from others.

My basic principles, values, and beliefs have been instilled in me from a Navajo man, my late grandfather, Betonnie Tsosie Begay II and my late grandmother, Zhonnie Chee Begay. My grandfather's character influenced me immensely. Through him, the Navajo culture taught me to listen, to have an open mind, and to be patient. I was constantly reminded that whatever I was doing at the time it would shape my life in the future, and that I will be able to build on self-sufficiency. My childhood consisted of being outside and having close relationships with the animals and land environment. My grandfather not only taught me ways of life, but he also used harsh discipline. My grandfather's farming tools have great meaning for me as they helped me recollect every inch of my childhood upbringing.

The hard work of planting, building and sewing the leather for the horse harnesses, preparing the horses and wagon for wood hauling, attending to the herd of sheep and cattle, planting, and sharpening the blades for cutting the hay to last for the upcoming winter—all this disciplined work developed strength within me. During these processes, I would be by his side listening to the rock wheel. Not only was this my playground, but it was also my work at a young age. I could still hear him say, "My child, someday you are going to be a leader and understand that being a leader in an organization is only temporary. You are to prepare and re-organize the organization for the next leader" (Betonnie Tsosie Begay III, personal communication, May 1975).

My late grandmother, Zhonnie Chee Begay taught me the importance of being a woman at a young age. Her character nourished me to who I am today. Her teachings were not all that harsh, but they were direct about home chores; often I was reminded of being a role model for the future generation by being respectful, kind, generous, and thankful to all who enter our home. Offering a warm gentle handshake and sharing all my four clans to all who enter was a priority. My four clans are, I am born for Coyote Pass People, born into Bitter Water People, my maternal grandparents are Water Edge People, and my paternal grandparents are Red Bottom People. My grandmother's priority was to educate me on the clanship and remember, her saying, "I am going to tell you once and you better remember and never forget", this phrase not only disciplined me, but back in the day, if we forget what was taught, there were consequences. I was given a lesson one evening during winter at our winter camp, after all the chores were completed, the chores included bringing in the sheep to the corral and having all the lambs placed with their appropriate birth mother, putting buckets of snow on the stove to melt overnight for the next day's cooking, taking the meat to the outside storage box that was located in the nearby tree, away from the animals, and laying out the bedding for the night for grandfather, grandmother, uncle, and myself. Once I completed this task, grandmother says, "sit down and listen". She started off with putting on some cedar and indicated that what I am going to share with you, you will use as a basic tool for your children, grandchildren, and individuals you will interact with in your day-to-day life. The cedar was for me to remember and never forget. She explained the reason I have my four clans and it started with my first clan; Coyote Pass People is from your mother's Clan group.

Coyote Pass is not necessarily coming from Navajo. It is from the Jemez Pueblo Indians. My mother's, late mother grandmother was part of the Long Walk and during the Long Walk, my great, great grandmother was taken from the group of Navajos, during the long walk, meaning she was stolen and after many months with the Pueblos and some Apache's, she somehow escaped, and made it back to the Navajo land. This not only happened to her but to several women and children and my great, great grandmother was part of this group. Coyote Pass People just adopted this clan from the Jemez Pueblo, and my grandmother stated that I am not really a Navajo, but a Jemez Pueblo Indian. Our elders also interpreted this clan as the Coyote People Clan are the strong and resilient people, they can withstand anything that comes their way and can overcome challenges in life.

Next is my second clan, which is my father's clan, Bitter Water People Clan. Bitter Water People Clan is the first of the four main clans that came from the Navajo's. Bitter Water People Clan survived with Water, their trail back from the Long Walk, they took many different paths through water streams, lakes and even rivers that kept the enemies away and enemies lost track of the Navajos. Navajos knew that water was one of the elements to survival.

My third Clan is my maternal grandfather's Clan, the Water Edge People Clan. This Clan was also named after the Water of survival. Our people felt safe camping near the water and water was used for drinking, cooking food, and cleaning.

My fourth clan is my paternal grandfather's Clan, the Red Cheek People Clan. The Red Cheek People Clan was created for healing. Many of my people suffered during the Long Walk and the Red Cheek People sought and located many different plant herbs for healing. Navajos suffered from broken bones; dislocations; heat; exhaustion; cuts; bruises; frost bites; headaches; backaches; and traumatization in experiencing constant rape, incest, and sudden deaths of family and relatives from elders to youth. The Red Cheek People healed and knew how to cope with trauma, and they explained the cycle of life that part of life is to experience such. The Red Cheek People Plan not only gathered plants, but they also created healing chants and prayers to the four sacred directions. This is what I remember and I will not forget the lesson.

The lesson of Clanship is heartfelt and is much respected by our people, but not well practiced by my own people. As I continue to practice the basic principle in using K'e, and following the friendly warm welcome and introductions of people, it was time to prepare a meal for the guest, even if it was a cup of coffee and a hot fry bread. My grandmother's cultural teachings include preparing traditional herbs, meals, and wool for weaving. These teachings brought many lessons on how to be independent and self-sufficient as a Navajo female.

My personal background and experiences started in a home with no running water and electricity. At a young age, in school my last name, Begay, was criticized by my peers and I was bullied by the students who poured salt in my hair during lunch time which caused me to have white hair at a young age. The students were cruel by calling me names of being gay from the name, "Begay" and being an old lady with white hair. I had done my best in avoiding these negative statements, and it only strengthened my desire to become a leader someday. It was brought to my attention by my late grandfather that someday I would hold a leadership position, would encounter various changes in leaders in an organization, and would have to adjust and adapt to changes. As my grandfather made this statement, my grandmother rudely interrupted and indicated that, "A Navajo woman is not to lead and this is what we were taught by our elders and leaders of the Navajo tribe" (Zhonnie Chee Begay, personal communication, May 1975). She strongly indicated that my responsibility as a woman was within the home. As my grandfather had stated, if I did ever become a leader, I was to understand that it was temporary, and that I was responsible in realigning the organization for a new leader.

Not only was I educated of being a leader and one priority from my paternal and maternal grandparents were as a Navajo woman, you are to model your leadership of charge and to be a peacemaker, if there is ever a conflict, and during your peacemaking, you are to always start with appropriate greeting and offer positive gestures, building this positive environment will build respect among all and you have a more clear outcome and solution to the conflict. The secret to the proper greeting is not only to all that is involved, but to the deities that are listening to your words and the observation they are making through the mysterious ways of enlightening to the deities. My paternal and maternal grandparents indicated that you will not be alone, you will be guided in a mysterious way, so I was to be clear, gentle, and have compassion.

Today, I am living out these predictions. In creating an environment using K'e is one of our basic principles that guides us in our different forms of life. K'é is our custom and tradition that builds respect among one another. K'é builds positive relationship with our people and the environment around us. When we use K'é within our communities it does represent Hózhó. Hózhó means to have harmony and peace.

As we rebuild on our basic principles of using K'é with harmony and peace, these teachings are to be re-taught from our home, known as our Navajo female Hogan. The Navajo female Hogan and its aspects of Mother Earth and Father Sky serve as lenses through which to understand and explore the characteristics of our Navajo people's inspiration, self-direction, planning, human relations, communication, motivation, and self-awareness. The Navajo female Hogan is our foundation of the many teachings that are instilled in us by our elders. As I remember during my puberty ceremony, and becoming part of the womanhood, it was engrained in me that being Navajo woman, that all the teaching we teach from your home represents not only you, but your elders, parents, and community. This foundation not only lays out the core elements of life, but you as an individual woman takes these elements to the next teaching level using fire, water, and air. It was drilled into me that I am not alone in this world and if there is ever a challenging time in life, you come back to your foundation and realign yourself with Mother Earth and Father Sky.

The Navajo Female Hogan is sacred because it originated from Mother Earth and Father Sky. The origination consists of our four sacred cardinal directions, the sacred mountains, sacred Mother Earth seasons, and the sacred colors of the Navajo Female Hogan. According to our forefathers' understanding and beliefs, Mother Earth is our mother. What our mother is dressed with is what we are dressed with from the bottom of our feet to the top of our heads. She makes us aware and acknowledges our sacred footsteps on her flesh and body, which is the main purpose of being on this earth. The earth is our mother, so as Navajo people, we address the earth as our Mother Earth.

Mother Earth was founded from our four directions, sacred mountains, sacred seasons, and sacred colors of the Navajo Female Hogan. According to the story of our forefathers, the great creation of the four directions took place when light, air, water, and earth were made. The Holy People created the four directions. Our forefathers believed that the sacred directions have a spiritual knowledge and discipline for us. We were instructed to understand each direction. Mother Earth consists of the four sacred directions beginning with East known as the Early Dawn Spirit. This is where our thoughts, thinking, and physical fitness are initiated with great mental strength for a better today, tomorrow, and future. Next, the South is known as the Blue Twilight Spirit. This is where the planning and preparation are initiated with good knowledge and wisdom. Third, the West is known as the Yellow Evening Twilight Spirit. This is where Iina was created with old age of life combined with courage and health for our minds. The North is known as the Spirit of Folding Darkness. This is where happiness is initiated with compassion and satisfaction of all beings.

The Holy People use the sacred soil that First Man brought up from the lower worlds and replanted the four sacred mountains. The sacred mountains are Blanca Peak from the East, which represents Thinking; Mount Taylor from the South, which represents Planning; San Francisco Peak from the West, which represents Necessity of Life; Mount Hesperus from the North, which represents Future Happiness; Gobernador Knob from the Northeast, which represents Love; and Mount Huerfano from the Northeast, which represents Faith.

The sacred seasons were divided after the divine of the Holy People finished the creation of the sun and moon. First Man and First Woman thought about growing plants and insects, animals, and birds. They even thought about when they should give birth and when they should plant and harvest. It was then decided that the seasons be divided into four parts and would start with spring; this was the planting season, and plants would begin to grow. During the summer the plants would ripen and be harvested. Fall time the pollen and seeds would fall to the ground to create life to the full extent and will end with winter, where frost is created, and the Holy People would await the sound of Lightning People for an early spring.

The Navajo Female Hogan was made for the purpose of a place for resting, to eat, a place to talk and laugh, a place where children can be born and can grow. Talking God instructed First Man how to build a Female Hogan after the emergence and was given the sacred minerals for the foundation. The Navajo Female Hogan had four posts and each post had its representation. The East post represents White Shell, the South post represents Turquoise, the West post represents Abalone Shell, and the North post represents Black Jet. The Holy People instructed all human beings to keep this Hogan clean at all times and not to conduct any ceremonies in the Hogan. Our forefathers addressed this Navajo Female Hogan as a mother, because it takes care of you like a mother does. The Navajo Female Hogan is built with humble thoughts and prayers. The Hogan is a home where a mother and father begin their teachings and all relatives are welcomed and many teachings are echoed. After the Hogan is built the official dedication of the Female Hogan begins with a prayer using the white corn, yellow corn, and corn pollen. The corn is sprinkled in the four directions and throughout the Hogan. After the completion of the dedication, Grandfather Fire is brought into the Hogan, followed by Fire Poker to serve as protection for the family. As once stated by my grandfather, "If your mother or father dies at an early age, you will realize the value of your Hogan and what it stands for."

The four sacred colors in the inner circle of the Navajo Female Hogan include Yellow, Turquoise, Blue, and White, which all contribute to becoming a Navajo woman. These colors represent different nourishment and development of womanhood. The color yellow represents infancy to 25 years old. During this time, you are born and introduced to the Navajo Female Hogan as to how you will carry yourself into womanhood. Next, Turquoise represents 26 to 50 years of age and all materialistic things that will increase your awareness of womanhood. Third, Blue represents 51 to 75 years of age and the reflection of your upbringings from a young age. Fourth, White represents 76 to 102 years of age and shows the knowledge and wisdom that the woman has gained in time. The Navajo Female Hogan is our mother and our forefathers who indicated that all living creatures were made to have a home and our Mother Earth's home is the parts of the directions, mountains, seasons, and colors as the roof of our home.

Father Sky is also sacred and in support of female development, Father Sky offers many teachings that are taught again after having been introduced from Mother Earth. Father Sky is a spiritual sense and provides the natural attitude and our pattern of behaviors. Father Sky controls our spiritual laws and makes us understand our dos and don'ts. His responsibility is to enforce all teachings and to lay out any consequences if laws are violated. According to the teachings of our forefathers, in order to understand your Hogan, you have to understand the nature of the earth, all the teachings of the nature of the earth come from Mother Earth and Father Sky to help you understand your home environment. As Diné people we consider the world to be holy and sacred including our Hogan and the environment. In today's generation, we have become more accustomed to instant answers and different entertainment. For this reason, we are not aware of our behaviors, attitudes, beliefs, and values.

Navajos view the environment with a holistic view that emphasizes beauty, peace, joy, and harmony. The spiritual learning is sacred and makes us unique. According to Aronilth (1991), the story of our forefathers, the great creation of the four directions took place when light, air, water, and the earth were made. The Holy People created the four directions. Our forefathers believed that the sacred four directions had a spiritual knowledge and discipline for us. We must understand all forms of the four directions, as matter represent the same intelligence that is in us. We are part of it. We, as the Navajo people, must recognize that this intelligence is ours to draw upon, to understand, and to use. The four directions are the foundation and spirit of our thinking and intelligence.

As my late grandfather instilled in me at a young age, the four sacred cardinal directions represent the following. First, from the East is thinking with the sacred stone of white shell. Second, from the South is planning, with the sacred stone of turquoise. Third, is from the West, which is socializing with the stone of abalone shell. Fourth, from the North, is to believe that all will be well with the stone of black jet. This message was used for everyday prayers and chants. The directions also embed the use of K'e. As we greet our directions, we are educated to properly address them, using K'e. When this is used the deities listen to your voice and carries out the blessing for you to survive on Mother Earth and I could hear my grandfather, "My child, always call out the cardinal directions in the proper order, and with this order, it will lead you to many successes in life, not only are you going to call out in this order, but to properly greet them with how you were taught by your elders" (Betonnie Tsosie Begay III, personal communication, May 1975). K'e is not only used to introduce yourself to others in Navajo language but is a basic leading tool that will guide you to embrace the abundance of a joyful life.

K'e Human relations are important to individuals and/or groups of people. Human relations can impact costs, competitiveness, and the long-term economic sustainability of a business. I believe that modeling positive working relationships reduces employee turnover, increases productivity, and fosters creativity. Building positive relationships, recognizing an individual's value, and expressing concern for his or her need often goes a long way. Human relations are not only practiced by adults, but with young children as well. Growing up in a rural area with no running water and electricity on the Navajo reservation led to an understanding of human relations when speaking to the Navajo elders in their Navajo language.

To model and practice this greeting is the key to understanding human relations. Human relations not only shape who you are but require you to have a full understanding of traditional Navajo practices. With that said, achieving success through effective communication results from successful collaborative experiences using K'e. Individuals who communicate effectively in using K'e often work well together on projects, communicate ideas, and provide motivation in getting things done. The benefits of effective communication involve stronger decision-making, increased productivity, stronger business relationships, enhanced professional images, improved stakeholder responses, and quicker ways to solve problems.

The spirit of our clans tells us that our children, our family, and our people need to be recognized for who they are. According to our forefathers' teachings, we need to know who we are. We need to answer questions like, "what clan am I?" We need to know about the race from which we come, and we need to know why our color of skin and our language are different. According to Aronilth (1991), we are positively identified as a Diné. We are given this name at the time that we were created by the Holy People. For this reason, we are told that when we say, "I am Diné" we are saying, "I am the child of the Holy People." Diné means children of the Holy People, child of the Holy People.

As the lens of an effective leader through the Navajo cultural teachings, the four themes of vision, k'e human relations, and communication lead to a better understanding of each Navajo individual. As a woman leader, once I create a vision, I will focus and follow through with using the proper clanship system that will build a positive relationship and communication for my community and the workplace. I remember an employee saying to me, how do you know how to greet an individual and was impressed with me using my clanship in greeting individuals. Once I used the proper greeting to the individual, I immediately received a warm smile and received respect, especially from elderly. Elderly Navajo often would like to speak with someone that is fluent in the Navajo language and know that they will get the assistance they need by communicating with one that speaks fluently in the Navajo language. As I greet them as Shima, they in return will greet me as Shi'yazhi or sha'awee, which them means that I am going to do my best in getting them what they need assistance with.

Using K'e in proper greeting also comes from appreciating nature. There are teachings that I do take for granted. At a young age, my focus was always livestock and outside chores, and I did not appreciate nature. It was most likely brought to my attention, and I ignored it. I often wonder how I would be today, as a woman in knowing all the plant herbs that will heal my people. I did not have to go to school to know the herbs and it was right there in front of me, and boy, did I lose out on this. I do tell myself, that this only happened for a reason, as my paternal grandfather would say. Today, I know very little of traditional plant herbs and realized, until I got older that nature is medicine and nature does heal. Nature was and has been always part of the key element of survival. As we introduce our selves to one another using our four clans in K'e, the plant life also has their clans and their clans have feelings, just as we have our senses, our plants live from season to season as we do. This is why it is important to know who you are and know where you come from. It is about your own self-awareness. My maternal grandmother indicated, "Whenever you make a mistake, people are not going to see who you are, they are going to say, "who is her mother? where does she come from? who are her grandparents? and don't they teach her the basic principles?", so be aware of yourself and know your surroundings.

I was taught that in life you will encounter challenges and when this occurs, that you turn to nature, go home, and speak to nature, they listen, and they will guide you in making sound decisions. As sounds of wind, sun, winter, breeze of cold air, and plants waving means to turn to them, they have answers for you and guide you toward the directions for protection. Directions are from the seasons, and no one listens to them or sees what they create in the sunlight or darkness. Prior to the COVID-19 pandemic, nature knew and was trying to signal to the human being, there is something approaching into the world and that we were to take cover from this something that was evil and may destroy lives. No one knew and very few traditional practitioners sought guidance on steps to take. The clouds and the unusual colors from the sun close to dawn showed us what was coming to our mother earth and father sky, when this was seen by very few, very few began to take cover and exactly 4 months later, the pandemic hit our tribal nation. If we were all aware of surroundings and took self-awareness seriously, more lives would have been saved. We lost many during the pandemic and as a leader, I was part of doing my best in using my Navajo language and Ke' to save lives. Our elders were appreciative in hearing the K'e and the precautionary measures in the Navajo language. As I continue to talk about the pandemic, I did not realize how big of an impact it had on my people and most of my Navajo people returned home and embrace nature by using herbal plants as medicine for healing. Many traditional songs and prayers were also part of the nature and nature listened and guided us all to heal. Today, we are still healing and using nature and plants for healing and guidance. As speaking to plants and nature, it is becoming a habit of our own self-awareness.

Self-Awareness is about understanding your own needs, desires, failings, and habits. The more you know about yourself, the better you are at adapting to life changes that suit your needs. The more you pay attention to your emotions and how you work, the better you will understand why you do the things you do. Self-awareness is being conscious of what you are good at while acknowledging what you have yet to learn. One benefit of self-awareness is that you see that pretending that you know everything when you do not creates further problems. On the other hand, if you can take responsibility for what you do not know, you benefit yourself and your institution by calling for additional learning or expertise. Another area related to self-awareness is respecting others. Wanting to be treated with respect means understanding that you also must give the other respect. Self-awareness is having a clear perception of your personality, including strengths, weaknesses, thoughts, beliefs, motivation, and emotions. Self-awareness allows an individual to understand other people and how you are perceived. According to Turner (1995), many believe they live in self-trust when in fact they live in independency. People depend on their families or their careers in feeling security.

Our forefathers said the *Sa'ah Naaghai Bike'Hozhoon* is the root and foundation of the teaching of our philosophy, beliefs, learning, lifestyle, language, and values. These were already created, established, and developed by *Sa'ah Naaghai Bike'Hozhoon* (SNBH) through the minds of our Holy People. The discipline of SNBH makes us understand that we seek the way with SNBH. We will not waste a moment in life or question SNBH for it is a natural process of life. With this philosophy of the Holy People in our minds and thoughts, we can reach a new horizon with a clear understanding of ourselves.

About the Author

Dr. Perphelia Fowler, a fluent Navajo speaker, serves as the Human Resource Director for Diné College in Tsaile, Arizona. Dr. Fowler has extensive human resources expertise and before returning to Diné College, she served as a cabinet member, under the Nez/Lizer Administration for the Navajo Nation Division of Human Resources in Window Rock, Arizona. Previously, she served in various human resources positions with Navajo Technical University and Red Mesa Unified School District. She earned her Doctorate Degree in Educational Leadership for Change from the Fielding Graduate University in Santa Barbara, California; Master's Degree in Human Resources-Business Administration; and Bachelor's Degree in Human Resources-Business Administration.

References

American history from revolution to reconstruction and beyond. Navajo Treaty 1868, Fort Sumner, New Mexico, June 1, 1868. Retrieved November 6, 2015 from http://www.let.rug.nl/usa/documents/

Aronilth, W., Jr. (1991) *Foundation of Navajo culture.* Tsaile, Navajoland, USA: Diné College.

Diné cultural standards for students. (1999). *Office of Diné Culture, Language, and Community Service, Division of Diné Education.* Window Rock, AZ: Record Management Center

Wheatley, M. (2006). *Leadership and the new science: Discovering order in a chaotic world* (2nd ed.). San Francisco, CA: Berret-Koehler.

Young, M. (2015). Native women move to the front of tribal leadership: Native daughters. Retrieved November 3, 2014 from http:// www.cojmcunl.edu/ nativedaughters/leadership/html

AFTERWORD: THINKING FOR THE FUTURE

Becoming Modern-Day Warriors Through Education

Dr. Buu Nygren, President
The Navajo Nation

I came from very humble beginnings, growing up at Yellow Rock Point, Utah, also known as Red Mesa due to the towering plateau that defines the landscape. Raised by my mom and grandma, I grew up in a family that deeply valued education despite not having the opportunity to pursue it themselves.

My mother faced a challenging life. She gave birth to me during her freshman year of high school, causing her to leave the 9th grade and never return. Raising me alone without my father, whom I never met, was a struggle. Our home was a 14-foot travel trailer with a propane stove and a routine of hauling water. My grandmother attended the Sherman Indian School in Riverside, California, but only briefly, leaving after the 2nd grade and never returning.

Despite their hardships, the greatest gift my mother and grandmother gave me was the belief that education was my path to a better future. My mother always said that high school would not be enough; for my future security and happiness, I needed to achieve higher education. "Son, you're going to have to do something we've never done in the family," she said. The world beyond Yellow Rock Point demanded it.

As a young boy, I decided that I had to excel. I saw how hard it was for my mother to drive 70 miles one way to work various low-paying jobs in Farmington, New Mexico, and return to take care of me each day.

Since childhood, she would say, "What are you going to do if I'm not here? Nobody's going to help you. You need to know how to help yourself." She always meant education. So I worked at it. I was promoted from my middle school as salutatorian. In high school, my goal was always to come in first, whatever the challenge. At some point, I decided I wanted to go to Arizona State University. I didn't know what I wanted to study. I just knew that ASU was where I would find the education and tools to achieve what my mother and grandmother envisioned for me. I worked hard and graduated as valedictorian of Red Mesa High School, earning the Navajo Nation's Chief Manuelito Scholarship, the Gates Millennium Scholarship, and others that made college affordable.

Discovering My Path

I began ASU in 2006 to pursue an aerospace engineering degree. Later, I changed my major to civil engineering. Despite my love for math, my favorite subject, those majors weren't for me. During high school, my uncles taught me how to build. I started with sheds, doghouses and outhouses, eventually framing houses. To my surprise, I learned that ASU offered a degree in construction management and technology. With that, I found my focus.

Coming from such a remote place on the Navajo Nation, I've been asked what impressed me most about moving to Phoenix for college. Leaving home after high school is often frightening for Navajo kids, leading many to finish a semester, go home, and not return. It wasn't like that for me. I thrived.

The one thing that impressed me most as a new student was the freedom to take a shower whenever I wanted and stay under that stream of water for as long as I wanted. It was a simple luxury that so many take for granted but that many Navajo students never had. It made me wonder, what else could this new world offer?

When I graduated from Arizona State, I knew that through education, I could always figure out what would come next. I've always found that to be true of education. Whether learning to be a carpenter, fixing my own vehicle, or figuring out complex problems, education was my key to self-reliance.

Lifelong Learning

Looking back from 2024, my life journey embodies the concept of lifelong learning. Never stop learning. Today, my message to high school and college students is that is the only way to help yourself, to learn and keep learning, and I'm still doing that. Because if you're not willing to learn, you're going to be left behind, and I never wanted to be left behind. That was the scariest thought I could imagine; being left behind while the world moves on.

No matter what it took, I tried to do my very best. In my undergraduate years, I didn't have the highest GPA, but I had the determination to never quit. As hard as it was, challenge after challenge, I believed in myself and was not going to let myself down. That's what's important about education. It's a solo sport, and whether you're first or last, what matters most is that you finish.

Becoming a Modern-Day Education Warrior

We are told our great-great-grandfathers and grandmothers left us this great Navajo Nation because they always adapted to their situation. When our people acquired horses, their world expanded. They could better feed and protect themselves. They became more independent and fierce warriors. When the Spaniards arrived, they adapted to silversmithing, acquired better horses and breeds of sheep. For the last 100 years, Navajos have become world-renowned for their arts, skills, ingenuity, work ethic and continue to adapt.

Once, the Navajo Tribe had only one lawyer. He was our former Navajo Tribal Chairman Thomas Dodge, son our first chairman Henry Chee Dodge and brother to renowned council delegate Annie Dodge Wauneka. Chairman Dodge graduated from the St. Louis University Law School in 1932 and served as tribal chairman from 1933 to 1936. Today, the Navajo Nation Bar Association has more than 300 active members and hundreds more Navajo men and women are practicing law at firms around the country.

Similarly, there were no Navajo doctors until 1958. Dr. Taylor McKenzie earned his medical degree that year and went on to have a distinguished career in public and Indian health. Dr. McKenzie became Navajo Nation Vice President McKenzie in 1999. Following that, he was appointed the Navajo Nation's first medical officer in 2005.

Today, there are many Navajo doctors, lawyers, and those with master's and doctoral degrees in many fields. Two generations ago, Navajo education led only to trade schools and secretarial programs because we were considered better with our hands than we were with our minds. How is it that the children of those Navajo students, who were thought by their BIA boarding schoolteachers to be mentally deficient because they wouldn't look them in the eye or speak when spoken to, have succeeded so spectacularly in so short a time?

I suggest two reasons. First, since returning from the Long Walk with the "Old Paper," the Navajo people held onto their language, culture and teachings while adapting to a foreign world. Second, once Navajos adapted, we've made education and the worlds it takes us to our own. Success brings success. Success boosts confidence. Confidence inspires self-belief. Self-belief motivates to take on more goals and challenges. And the skills and experience that come with that bring yet further success and greater happiness.

Wherever I go, I tell students of all ages to reflect on what they've done, both successes and failures. Then move on and get better. After receiving my BS, I worked in construction for 10 years. Eventually, I wanted to come home, so I returned to ASU to earn an MBA. When I enrolled for my doctorate at the University of Southern California, I was working a fulltime job with Navajo Engineering and Construction Authority, arriving on the job at 7 a.m. after getting up at 3 a.m. to study every day. Even now, as Navajo Nation president, I eagerly want to learn to figure out how to get more tools to help myself so I can help my people. Along the way, I've discovered I am moved to serve.

I remind students that if they can't help themselves, they can't help anyone. But first they need to believe in themselves. They need to believe they are more than capable. They need to believe that mindset is tied to all their successes.

The Warrior's Despondency

In every warrior story in every culture through the ages—from Odysseus in the Odyssey, Aragorn in The Lord of the Rings to our own Chief Manuelito—the warrior confronts moments of despondency. These are filled with discouragement, hopelessness, confusion, and despair. These are universal stories, mirrored in our own Navajo traditions and teachings. They depict the struggle between right and wrong, good and evil, old and new, and especially success and failure. These stories are powerful metaphors for the personal inner conflicts we all face. They teach that each of us, especially as students who occasionally feel that hopelessness, is engaged in an internal struggle in life, just like the heroes of these epic tales.

At the heart of these stories is the hero. This can be anyone, man or woman, like Changing Woman or Spider Woman. The hero embodies courage, resilience, and skill in the struggle. They find a way to triumph, becoming a symbol of strength and leadership. The hero's virtues – bravery, loyalty, and self-sacrifice – inspire and guide others to take action. True leadership requires action, encompassing tactics, proficiency, strategic thinking, and the will to overcome adversity. This principle holds whether on the high school football field, applying to college, launching a business, or leading the Navajo Nation.

We know our Navajo ancestors and leaders faced hopelessness and despondency from the time of the Long Walk when they strove to protect the people under their care. Today's Navajo education warriors are our heroes. Schools are the boot camps and education is the training that forges our Modern-Day Navajo Warriors. Like our ancestors wielding shields, spears, bows, and arrows against superior forces, our Modern-Day Warriors may battle inner and outer struggles but succeed armed with the power of education.

I, too, struggled. I knew I wasn't naturally gifted in many areas. The only thing I consistently excelled in was math. Math was my sanctuary. Whenever I took a math class, I felt at ease. The one other subject I enjoyed as much was history, particularly American history, because it was storytelling.

Reading was a challenge for me, too, possibly because I spoke two languages. When told something in Navajo, I would remember it vividly, like a picture, because of the descriptive nature of our language. Comprehending English was more difficult. It didn't translate in my mind the same way. Over the years, I practiced and practiced. There were times as a student when I simply had to overcome it and learn. I had to conquer my despair and despondency like an education warrior.

Being the father of two young girls, reading is now a daily part of our family life. It wasn't like that when I was growing up. Every morning, our two-and-a-half-year-old runs to me with her picture book, eager for me to read to her in both English and Navajo, depending on the book. Our house is filled with Navajo language children's books.

I read to both her and our five-month-old in English and Navajo. To Jasmine and me, it's crucial that our daughters hear both languages. As the world outside of Navajo accelerates and becomes more competitive, equipping the younger generation, in this case my daughters, with the best tools sets them up for success. It's a fact that those who learn the most will be more competitive, especially in complex fields like science, technology, engineering, mathematics, and computer science. Families and the Navajo Nation must ensure our students don't get left behind in terms of technology. As a Navajo leader with an eye on the future, this is my most significant focus.

I've been asked how much Navajo and English I use. Out of necessity, English dominates my discussions. The only times I primarily speak Navajo are when I'm around elders or during my weekly radio address. When I read books, I try to think in Navajo. If a book isn't translated into Navajo, I'll translate it for my kids. I strive to become more fluent every day.

When I was younger, all the way into my early 20s, I would dream and think in Navajo. That's because I was always around my grandma and relatives who spoke and thought in Navajo. As I adapted to living in Phoenix or Tempe and working in the Maricopa County area, my train of thought gradually shifted more to English.

Leading as a Modern-Day Education Warrior

My relatives tell stories of how, as a kid, I would gravitate toward any microphone and start speaking. Speaking in front of people came naturally to me.

When something is imprinted in my mind, or when a story is told to me, it's much easier for me to speak. When giving a speech, even if it's unscripted, I focus on the story and the "why" behind it.

I remember walking the halls of my junior high school, seeing portraits of Navajo Nation presidents and chairmen hanging in the hallways. I thought to myself, "Why not me? Could I be a chairman or president of the Navajo Nation? Could I lead my people, make them proud, make my community proud?" That's where my first thoughts of becoming president originated. I saw the dream. I envisioned it. It propelled me to prepare. I never shied away from speaking.

Today, after 18 months as president, the job is what I expected it to be. It's been an exciting time filled with many successes. We've initiated changes within the Navajo Nation. Seeing this growth and change is incredibly exciting. While I can see my vision taking shape, not everyone does.

When change occurs, people feel uncertain. They feel frustrated or doubtful. The way we've approached things and challenged everybody, we've made it clear that if you're going to meet with me, it needs to be about moving priorities and my agenda forward. I'm in a hurry and still hold on to the memory of not wanting to be left behind. There's a lot that needs to be done, and I want to do it. My staff and directors are my soldiers, my warriors. We confront the monsters of bureaucratic lethargy and Navajo poverty every day. We face monsters of hunger and despair. Failure is not an option. Our shields and spears are our educations. We face our opponents who want to hold us back. We stand our ground and move steadily forward, issue by issue.

We've achieved remarkable things in a year and a half. We have an Arizona water rights agreement in place with three tribes, the state, the federal government, and other parties. That is historically unprecedented. We've secured economic development with projects like the purchase of Goulding's Lodge at Monument Valley, a world-class tourist destination with 300 Navajo employees whose jobs are now secure. We've figured out how to use all $2 billion in ARPA funding from COVID-19 to set up a trust fund to leverage money so the Navajo Nation can borrow more to build infrastructure and grow. I call this "thinking for the future" and building our economic success on Navajo. Educated Navajo minds got us here.

Thinking for the Future as Modern-Day Education Warriors

We as Navajo leaders must begin to think and operate as if we are multi-billionaires developing a country. At this point in our history, we need to chart that path forward. Why not? Why can't we think like that? Why shouldn't we believe that we can be a strong, independent, economic powerhouse in the United States? I believe in it because the Navajo people are incredibly smart, capable, and knowledgeable. Despite repeated attempts to defeat us, we have always prevailed. I believe we can be better than all outside governments. I believe it is that time.

For 25 years, perhaps longer, Navajo elders have asked for young, educated Navajos to assume leadership positions. Now we have the first generation of young leaders running our government and making our laws. We have the most educated Navajo Nation Council in our history. We have the most educated executive branch.

We have leaders who use Western education while challenging themselves to remember where they come from. I've always tried to lead with this in mind. Although I followed my elders' instruction to obtain a bachelor's, master's, and doctorate, I try not to rely solely on my formal education. I think about our people who may have only a fifth grade education or secondary education yet possess profound knowledge, wisdom, and respectability. What would they do? What would they think? I try to combine both perspectives to avoid steering solely into Western thinking.

Seeing the growth and change in our Navajo government is exhilarating. It's exciting to witness a president who, despite being well-educated, remains down-to-earth and speaks and communicates in our own language in 2024. It's heartening to see a council with many members holding degrees and doctorates. This combination is crucial for Navajo leadership to function harmoniously and in the best interests of our people. We must ensure we do our homework and make decisions that truly benefit our people.

Reconciling Colonization and the Education Warrior Ethos

We must think not only of those who are living now but of those who haven't been born yet. For the past decade, discussions have focused on how Native American tribes have been colonized since European settlers arrived in North America. Native people across the country are pursuing higher education, succeeding as lawyers, doctors, scientists, educators, and tradespeople. Navajos excel in every field, with education as the cornerstone of our greatest achievements.

Everything I've advocated to students and adults is about retaining and using our language and culture. To remain a strong nation, we must hold onto this. If we do, we have done our part to avoid complete colonization. If you can speak your language, you will continue to be Navajo.

Navajos have always adapted while remaining true to our identity. We became silversmiths and are still among the best. We became rug weavers, unrivaled in our craft. We thrived as farmers and ranchers in our dry lands, raising millions of horses, cows, sheep, and goats. In the 1950s, 60s, 70s, and up to today, we became sought after welders across the country, incorporating the intrinsic spatial and kinesthetic skills known to our weavers, sand painters, and other artists.

Today, education has produced Navajo lawyers, judges, state legislators, doctors, scientists, chemists, hydrologists, mathematicians, CPAs, and investors. We have a robust body of Navajo Supreme Court decisions, and our judicial branch is renowned for its thoughtful opinions and impartiality. Navajos have always combined Western thinking with Navajo wisdom, continuously using our minds to thrive.

If we continue to hold onto our language and culture while integrating technology, I am excited to see what comes next. This is how we minimize the impact of complete colonization. Some may still view colonization as entirely negative, yet many of our people desire the amenities of modern civilization—access to a simple shower, the internet, online businesses, and more. We cannot completely escape the impact of colonization, as it shapes our future.

Navajos enjoy these modern amenities. Here's the thing: if you embrace being Navajo, you'll always be Navajo in a competitive world, and you will have an edge that few others possess. As Navajo leaders and influencers, to remain Navajo in a world of change and technology we must invest in saving and promoting our language.

Sovereignty and Thinking for the Future

If Navajos incorporate this mindset from preschool to elementary school, through high school and college, maintaining both Navajo and English, it will strengthen our young individuals' ability to process complex ideas and different types of learning. Bilingual thinking will enable them to adapt to various circumstances as they grow older. For our people to be successful, we need to pursue Navajo educational sovereignty. We must empower our students to learn, adapt and educate themselves using our language.

Ancient Wisdom in a Modern World
T'aa ho ajit'eego, "It's Up To You."

When it comes to our ancient wisdom, my mom would ask, "What are you going to do? Wait for others to do the work or do something about it?" All you can do is pray for strength, determination, and discipline to make it happen, and always believe in yourself. Whether you're in preschool or an adult, as long as our students have the sense that "I am good enough," that "I can do something good for myself and my family," and that they deserve it, they will succeed. That's what *t'aa ho ajit'eego* truly encompasses—you're worth it.

You must know that you're worth the education you deserve. You're worth the innovation, creativity, and thinking you want to pursue. You're worth it all, and you should pursue it. This will give you purpose in how you see yourself. That's the essence of *t'aa ho ajit'eego*—whatever path you take, know that you are on it with purpose, that you are capable, that you will be successful, and that you will continue on this path until we as a people are no longer here.

Today's Navajos are modern day warriors. Our successes demonstrate this. We've equipped ourselves with Western educational tools as well as our own teachings. We use these to fight the battles that threaten to undermine us. Yet, we are still here. One hundred years from now, 500 years from now, 1,000 years from now, we will stand before the dawn to say to our Holy Ones, "I am proud to be a Navajo."

About the Author

Dr. Buu Nygren, 37, was elected president of the Navajo Nation in November 2022. He took office on Jan. 10, 2023. He was raised by a single mother in Yellow Rock Point, Utah. He graduated valedictorian from Red Mesa High School in Red Mesa, Ariz. Loving to build, he earned a BS in Construction Management and Technology from Arizona State University, an MBA from ASU, and an Ed.D. in Organizational Leadership and Change from the University of Southern California. After 60 years of seeking tribal water rights, President Nygren's administration saw the Northeastern Arizona Indian Water Rights Settlement Act introduced in Congress in July 2024. If authorized, it will be the largest Indian water rights settlement ever approved. President Nygren and his wife Jasmine Blackwater-Nygren are the parents of two daughters.

Figure 1

Dr. Barbara Mink, Dr. Buu Nygren, and Rose Graham

Note. Dr. Buu Nygren, President of the Navajo Nation (center), with Dr. Barbara Mink (left) and Rose Graham (right). *(Photo by Barbara Mink).*

Appendix: Navajo Education Conferences

Held at the Navajo Nation Museum in Window Rock, Arizona, the **Annual Navajo Education Conferences** are a joint effort between Fielding Graduate University, the Navajo Nation, the Navajo Nation Department of Diné Education, the Office of Navajo Scholarship and Financial Assistance (ONNSFA), and Navajo Nation Teacher Education Consortium.

Figure 1. The 8th Annual Navajo Education Conference of 2024, featuring Department of Diné Education (DODE) Acting Superintendent Roy Tracy. *(Courtesy, Cody M. Begaye).*

First Annual Navajo Education Conference, June, 2017

Keynote speaker: Dr. Manley Begay, Northern Arizona University

Theme: Navajo Nation Building: Challenges and Hope for the Future

Sessions included such topics as:

• Toward Educational Sovereignty for the Navajo Nation: Structure, Curriculum and Quality

• Drum and Sing out the Language: An Action Research Study

• "Collapsing the Fear of Mathematics: A Study of the Effects of Navajo Culture on Navajo Student Performance in Mathematics

Second Annual Navajo Education Conference, April, 2018

• Welcome Address by Navajo Nation President Jonathan Nez.

• Keynote by Dr. Tommy Lewis, Navajo Nation Superintendent of Schools, on "Using Educational Research to Advance Quality Education on the Navajo Nation"

• Dr. Elmer Guy, President of Navajo Technical University presented on "The Role of Higher Education in Job Creation and Economic Sovereignty"

Third Annual Navajo Education Conference, April, 2019

• Welcome Address by Navajo Nation President Jonathan Nez.

• Dr. Perphelia Fowler, Executive Director of Navajo Nation Office of Human Resources, presented on: "Navajo Female Leaders: Weaving Together Their Experiences, Culture and Community"

• Dr. Sherry Allison, President of Southwestern Indian Polytechnic Institute, facilitated a panel of Higher Education leaders on: "Student Success is Everyone's Business"

• Mr. Gerardo Tunumbala, co-founder of Misak University, Columbia, South America attended the Conference from Columbia to present on: "To Recover the Land in Order to Recover Everything: The Plan of the Misak of Columbia to Decolonize Education."

During the pandemic, Annual Conferences were held virtually via ZOOM.

All virtual conferences were very well attended by Navajo teachers and leaders as well as by others interested in learning more about Indigenous ways of learning and leading.

2021

The publishing of the book, "The Future of Navajo Education" occurred in 2021.It was an innovative project that brought together the work of many who presented at the annual virtual Navajo Education Conferences including chapters by then Navajo President Jonathan Nez, The Honorable Chief Justice Emeritus Robert Yazzie, DODE Interim Superintendent Patricia Gonnie, and Northern Arizona University Professor Dr. Manley Begay. "The Future of Navajo Education" book was reviewed in the Winter 2022 issue of the *Tribal College: Journal of American Indian Higher Education.*

Sixth Annual Navajo Education Conference, July 2022

Sessions included such topics as:

- Enhancing Navajo Culturally Relevant Education for Head Start Children
- The Transformative Influence of Stories in the Lives of Navajo Women
- Healing Empowerment Through the Language Lineage Tree

Seventh Annual Navajo Education Conference, June 2023

Welcome by the Office of Navajo Nation President Dr. Buu Nygren.

Session topics included:

- Living Holistically: Practicing the Navajo Principles of Hozho and K'e with Dr. Miranda J. Haskie
- Enjoyability is Essential to Learning: Nitsáhákees, Nahat'á, Iina, and Siihasin with Dr. Telletha Valenski
- Cultivating Grit, Growth Mindset, and Self-Efficacy in Pre-Adolescent Navajo Students with Dr. Viola Hoskie
- Using the Indigenous Concept of Taa Who Aji T'eego T'eiya, Ya'at eehgo Ji Nahleh in Financial Literacy Curriculum Design for Navajo Students with Dr. Maxine Sloan
- Advancing Academic and Social Inclusion for Students with

Disabilities with Dr. Amanda Jackson

• Broadband Adoption, Tribal College Research and Education Network with Mr. Jason Arviso

Eighth Annual Navajo Education Conference, June, 2024

Welcome Address by Department of Diné Education (DODE) Acting Superintendent Roy Tracy

Session topics included:

• Tribal and Business Leaders' Perceptions of the Use of Broadband Internet Services on the Navajo Nation by Dr. Jason Arviso.

• Cultivating Grit, Growth Mindset, and Self-efficacy in Navajo Students by Dr. Viola Hoskie.

• Cultivating a Welcoming Environment for Gifted Navajo Students by Ms. Claudia Russell-Edgewater

• Navajo Grandparents Raising their Grandchildren: Their Strengths, Challenges and Needs by Dr. Delphina Dayish

• Using Indigenous Concepts in Financial Literacy Curriculum Design for Navajo Students, by Dr. Maxine Sloan

www.ingramcontent.com/pod-product-compliance
Lightning Source LLC
LaVergne TN
LVHW080454160826
845677LV00006B/1359

* 9 7 9 8 9 9 1 2 5 8 0 3 6 *